COLLEGE ADMISSIONS SIMPLIFIED

A Guide for the College-Bound

By Charlotte M. Klaar, PhD
with Mitchell St. Thomas

ISBN: 978-0-578-33384-7

Printed in the United States

To my students, past, present, and future:

Remember that success is determined by your dedication,
ability to recover from disappointments, and your sense of self!

CONTENTS

Foreword

I have a pretty clear memory of when and where I've met professional colleagues. I can picture a quick greeting outside of a busy exhibit hall, or a quiet conversation during a break in a training session. Sometimes my memory is strong because of a vigorous debate on college admission or an insight that left me wondering.

Yet, I have no specific memory of when I met Charlotte Klaar.

I think that is because within minutes of meeting Charlotte, you feel like old friends and colleagues. No time is needed to "warm up" to her, the warmth is there from the beginning. Her deep belief in colleagueship and sharing is on full display. Her knowledge of college admission is evident. And her commitment to helping adolescents through the college exploration process is as notable as it is infectious.

One might wonder "OK, she's warm and committed, but what's that have to do with a book on college admission?" And that is exactly why this book is so important.

College admission used to be clear and clean. Just a generation or two ago one would examine test scores and grades and be fairly certain which colleges would send the "fat envelope" and which the single page rejection letter. Those days—both of mailed envelopes and transparency—are long gone. The college process today is marked by dramatically lower acceptance rates, obscure bases for those getting in over others with similar records, and tuition that rivals the cost of the average American home. The changes keep coming: early decision, supplemental essays, common applications, test-optional among them. Yet the constant remains: with each change the process becomes less clear, and less predictable. Anxiety increases. Every parent may think their adolescent is a star and deserves admission everywhere, but teens today fear they'll get in nowhere. Stress has become a major concern among high schoolers as they launch their college search.

About now you could be wondering, 'so how does anyone help with such a confusing, opaque and ever-changing process'? And that's where Charlotte Klaar shines. She knows that a teenager cannot control a college admission officer's sometimes feckless decision, so she makes the process about what a student can do to assert control, increase personal awareness and gain a better understanding of themselves, their strengths and their interests.

Charlotte promotes, in this book and in her advising, that the college search and application process is a journey of self-discovery, of looking inward and coming out with wonderful options. Where the right fit—not a name brand—is the mark of success. Charlotte promotes the knowledge that a student succeeding and thriving wherever they go is the hallmark of success, and not the sticker on the back window of mom's Subaru.

To be sure, Charlotte has seen the college process and its changes up close. She has been a college advisor for nearly three decades, founding and running her own firms as an Independent Educational Consultant. In this capacity she has counseled, advised and supported hundreds of students ... celebrating that no two followed the same path.

In this book, Charlotte goes into the specifics of academics, extracurriculars, affordability, interviews, strategy & making oneself a unique and sought-after member of the incoming class. Yet, even as she spells out the specifics of how things work, how to craft the right essay and make the most of college visits, she never loses sight that it's about the student being true and authentic and finding the place that fits them like a custom-made collegiate sweatshirt.

Charlotte's ability to guide students and build her practices as an IEC has led her to be a frequently sought mentor by new college consultants in the Independent Educational Consultants Association. She served on the faculty of IECA's Summer Training Institute directly impacting the way 1,000 new IECs would see their role and build their own practices. Within IECA, the premiere organization representing professional college advisors, she chaired multiple committees, taught innumerable workshops and even led the Strategic Planning efforts to set out the future of the profession.

Charlotte often advises her IEC colleagues, just as she warns parents, that students must remain at the center of the college search. What this book does, more than anything, is keep to that simple equation: it's not about parents' egos, or where big sister attended, or advice from Uncle Jack or what will look good on a school's bulletin board. This process is about a student gaining a better understanding of themselves and the student—not parent or counselor—leading the research, the exploration and the decision-making. This book helps a family to put that teen front and center. Following the path set by Charlotte reduces family tension, adolescent anxiety and parent stress. This book is as much about maintaining family health as it is about choosing, applying to and matriculating at the right college.

I may not remember where or how or when I met Charlotte Klaar, but I know I'm lucky for having done so, as I have learned so much from her over the years—and through this book, you too can benefit from her knowledge, wisdom, and heart.

Mark Sklarow
Chief Executive Officer
Independent Educational Consultants Association

Hello, college-bound students (and your support staff). Thank you for buying this book and congratulations on your foresight to plan carefully for the college process. The process is not difficult, but it does require organization, planning, and—most importantly—a recognition of who owns the process. This last piece is what families typically find the most difficult to manage, considering the natural push and pull between parents and their teenagers. Further complicating that dynamic is the fact that the college choice and application process requires you—the student whose life will be affected by it—to be engaged and committed to its success, but rarely are you in control of the purse strings nor are you the one who is fully in control of the outcome. This book is meant to empower you to control what you can and to understand what constraints are put on you by finances and the whimsy of college acceptances.

Therefore, it's prudent that you and your parents establish the boundaries to be recognized between your activities and decisions and those that should belong to your parents. A common dividing line is that you will make all decisions except those that affect the family's finances, understanding that quite a few of the choices you'll make have a financial impact. Even in such a scenario, there is plenty of room for disagreement. Families should be prepared to resolve them through open discussion early in the process. I find it heartbreaking to have a student accepted to his/her dream school, only to be told that the family cannot afford it. That possibility should have been openly discussed *before* the application was ever submitted.

Success in admissions and the achievement of your educational goals are your family's *common* goals—and that's where I come in.

USING PARENTAL CONTROL

One of the most important responsibilities of American parents comes at the end of childhood. Your child, having prepared for college throughout high school, needs assistance in executing those tasks that will culminate in admission to colleges that are best suited to his/her needs and preferences. How much independence you have allowed your teenager to develop will have a significant impact on this journey. Many parents believe they have given their child ample opportunity to prove that s/he can make informed decisions, but, in fact, they have not. If you've made it a habit of rescuing your student from the consequences of their actions and blaming others for his/her lack of success, you have fostered dependence and whittled away at the self-confidence your child needs to make this a successful process.

As such, it might be a good time to step back and let a qualified Independent Educational Consultant shepherd your student. Students will benefit by having someone with an objective perspective advise them—someone who really hears what is being said—and when the college admissions results are received, s/he will know that the outcomes have been earned. The most difficult families for me are those who ignore what is best for their student and are simply trophy hunting. Parents, you will have to set your own egos aside and let your children find the colleges at which they can thrive academically amid a social setting that is accepting and validating.

ABOUT ME: I am a Certified Educational Planner with many years of experience. I have been in this business since 1995 and have loved every minute of it. My students become my own family for the 18 months or so that we work together. I learn about their fears, their successes, their failures, and their hopes. From what I learn about my students, I help them curate an application that is authentic and shows their uniqueness. Trust is built, and the results are good. My students own their process. My role is to manage the deadlines, to act as a sounding board for decisions, and to ensure that nothing is missed in this increasingly complex process.

My own background as the child of immigrant parents and the first in my family to attend college gives me a perspective that many others lack. I see education not only as a means out of poverty, but also as a gift that is to be treasured and nurtured. It is not a right; it must be earned. Because I needed to work to pay for my education, it took me 19 years to complete my bachelor's degree. Subsequently, I added a master's degree, a teaching certificate, and a PhD. My years of working with families and seeing how parenting changed with each child fascinated me and led to my doctoral focus on family systems. For this reason, my approach to this process is to find the right fit and match for each student.

MY MISSION: I am aware that, however useful the services of an Independent Educational Consultant may be, many families cannot or choose not to retain one. This book is for those families who see the value in an expert's proven methods but want to manage the college admissions campaign themselves. The book's aim is to help you realize that there is a college for everyone regardless of your socioeconomic status, cultural disadvantages, or anything else that you think is standing in your way. I have enabled many students to find colleges that further their academic growth *and* provide a campus culture that reflects their social needs.

HOW TO USE THIS BOOK: Ideally, parents and students will read the entire book to become familiar with all aspects of the admissions process, resulting in improved planning and coordination. As such, tips for parents will be scattered throughout the book. Simply look for this icon However, while parents play an important role, the preponderance of the work to be done in gaining admission to your "best-fit" colleges falls upon you, the student. If you're a high school sophomore or junior, I recommend that you read the entire book to better understand the challenges ahead of you. If you're a senior and time is short, check out The Cheat Sheet, beginning on page 5, for chapter overviews.

Best of luck to you all!
Charlotte M. Klaar, PhD

The Cheat Sheet: Chapter Overviews

In a hurry? If you don't have time to read the book in its entirety, here's a fast track to the topics covered in each chapter. As you proceed through the complexities of the college admissions process, be sure to check out the chapters/sections you need assistance with most to make your journey a successful one.

Chapter 1: How to Begin

As early as fall semester of sophomore year and no later than fall of junior year, you should contemplate and respond to the questions below. Your answers are likely to change, but this exercise sets a baseline going forward as you leap into the mechanics of admissions.

1. What are your goals for your education?
2. How would you describe your character?
3. What is the lifestyle that you aspire to have in the future?
4. What are your academic strengths and weaknesses?
5. What is the right field of study for you?
6. What are the career prospects in the field of study you are considering?
7. How do you see your future life?

Chapter 2: Affording College

For a generation, the costs of college have risen at a much faster rate than inflation, even though the number of students attending college has declined. As long as this situation persists, most families will need to find external sources of funds to help them pay for college.

Topics covered in this chapter include: the Free Application for Federal Student Aid (FAFSA), the CSS Profile, private scholarships, federal and state grants and scholarships, including National Merit Scholarships, US military grants and scholarships, institutional scholarships, and student loan programs. Other financial considerations, including changes to the FAFSA, which go into full effect for the 2024-2025 award year barring any further push backs to the date, with some provisions being phased in prior to that time, and how the American Rescue Plan (ARP) Act will impact you, are also summarized.

Chapter 3: Your Academic Record

Your academic record has three components: your Grade Point Average (GPA), your score on either the SAT or the ACT, and sometimes your class rank, if available.

Your GPA is a strong indicator of success in college and is considered more predictive than test scores or class rank. Hence, your GPA is the most important part of your academic record. However, the methods of calculating GPA by high schools and colleges isn't standardized.

Among the variables affecting your academic record are your grades in Advanced Placement (AP), International Baccalaureate (IB), and your high school's Honors courses. The positive impact of such courses should be weighed against any incentive you may have to raise your class rank, which remains a required admissions factor in a minority of colleges. Be careful in your course selection not to exceed your ability to produce good results. For those attending high schools that release class rank and who plan to apply to colleges that require it, strike a balance between aggressive course selection and the attainment of a great class rank.

Among the choices you'll need to make is which exam, SAT or ACT, plays to your strengths so that you'll achieve sufficiently high scores for the colleges you're targeting. This chapter summarizes the differences between the two tests and reviews the considerations that help you decide if you should apply via a test-optional plan.

Chapter 4: Your Extracurricular Activities

All college-bound students are aware from early in high school that colleges will assess their extracurricular activities as a factor in admissions. The best advice for your selection of extracurriculars is—more is *not* better. Depth is better. Colleges prefer a deep engagement in one or two activities above superficial participation in many. To advance your admissions prospects, commit wholeheartedly to activities that you genuinely enjoy, that improve your knowledge and skills, and that promote the greater good. How to choose extracurricular activities? First and foremost, the activity must be one that interests you, so what do you like to do with your time outside of the classroom?

There are certain activities that high school students assume will weigh heavily in their favor in admissions decisions. These include varsity sports, student government, performing arts, debate, and others. These are certainly worthy activities. But colleges want to assemble a diverse student body, so they seek applicants who possess a range of talents, skills, experiences, and characteristics. College administrators assume that such diversity will enhance the education of all students. Admission officers may be as impressed by a computer club member, homeless shelter worker, or job shift supervisor as they are by a class president or champion debater. They particularly favor applicants who are so outstanding in their field that they may one day reflect glory back upon their alma mater.

Chapter 5: Your Personal Preferences

There are many subjective, nonacademic factors that come to bear on the selection of the colleges that fit you best. These include such characteristics as geographic location, campus setting, student body size and profile, extracurricular opportunities, average class size, faculty involvement and mentorships, science labs, art studios, performance venues, cultural and recreational opportunities, transportation, climate, student diversity, and faculty-to-student ratio.

Chapter 5 will help you identify and prioritize the factors that are most important to you.

Chapter 6: Campus Visits

There is no substitute for being there. Nothing you do will tell you more about a college than a visit to its campus. A visit will reveal more useful information than its website, course catalog, statistical profile, media articles, and rankings publications put together. However, a successful college visit requires planning, so this chapter provides a protocol to follow that will make your visits more beneficial. By observing this method consistently, you'll be better able to compare colleges, apples-to-apples.

Chapter 7: Your College List

Your College List is the set of colleges that are exceptionally well suited to your needs, goals, and preferences as an individual. It's comprised of the institutions to which you'll apply in senior year and it's indispensable to the success of your admissions campaign.

In the previous chapters, we cover topics that are fundamental to building your College List. These include your educational goals, academic record, preferences, price range, and the results of your campus visits. Given this foundation, Chapter 7 will teach you how to construct a three-tiered College List of about 15 colleges that fit you best.

In building your College List, consider all types of institutions, including both public and private institutions, community colleges, military academies, technology and vocational institutes, large research universities, and small liberal arts colleges.

Chapter 8: Your Application—Strategy

Because admission is competitive, most colleges have adopted a holistic approach to analyzing applicants. As a result, admissions decisions rely not only on your academic record but on several non-quantifiable factors as well. These may include interviews, essays, letters of recommendation, and extracurricular activities, among others.

In order to present your best possible self to colleges, this chapter guides you in the development of an effective admissions strategy. One objective of your strategy is to determine how to distinguish yourself as an applicant. You should assess your strengths, accomplishments, and key personality traits in order to make the Admission Officer (AO) see you as you see yourself. Then decide which of your unique characteristics you want to stress in the application package. Once your strategy is established, you'll learn how to enhance your positive characteristics and emphasize them throughout your application in a clear, concise, and consistent manner.

Chapter 9: Your Application—Theme and Hooks

The principal means of communicating your strategy to colleges is through your theme. This is a brief statement of the reasons why you'll make an outstanding addition to a college's freshman class. The message will be woven throughout your application package so that AOs will perceive it clearly. Ideally, an AO will like it so much that s/he will use it to advocate for you in committee.

If you have a truly outstanding talent, aptitude, or skill, you have the makings of what's commonly referred to in the college admissions milieu as a hook. A hook will add to your appeal as an applicant beyond what you can expect from your academic record plus the soft admissions factors covered in previous chapters. A strong hook helps you get admitted to colleges that might otherwise be just out of reach for you. In addition to securing admission, a strong hook can provide you with scholarship offers to attend colleges that highly value what you have to offer.

In addition to athletes and performing artists, other freshman seats are awarded to applicants based on their hooks. Perhaps the hook with the greatest impact at private colleges is a legacy. This is an applicant whose grandparents, parent, or sibling is an alumnus of the institution. This applies only to those who received their bachelor's degree from the institution. If your parents or grandparents got their Masters, JD, or MD at the college, you are not a legacy. The total of successful hook applicants can account for up to 50 percent of a freshman class in a private institution. Some, but not all, would have been admitted solely on academic merit. There won't be a slacker among them, but their academic credentials aren't necessarily better than some applicants who were rejected, so the value of having a legacy hook is clear.

Chapter 10: Your Application—Essays

The quality of a student's essays is often the difference between acceptance and rejection. Academic records consist solely of quantitative data. They offer no means of distinguishing among students whose records are remarkably similar. To make a distinction, Admission Officers (AOs) rely more heavily on essays than on any other of the so-called soft factors: interviews, letters of recommendation, and extracurricular activities. This is one of the places that you become a "person" in the eyes of the AO rather than a folder with lots of numbers and little substance.

For strategic purposes, you should identify and emphasize special qualities that you possess to draw attention to your unique combination of talents, interests, and experiences. This is the type of characteristic that can elevate an AO's perception of you to where they consider you a better applicant than your academic peers.

The best ways to prove that you'll contribute positively to the school is by writing compelling essays. If you can make a gut-level connection with the AO reading it, you'll have an advantage over your competition.

Chapter 11: Your Application—Interviews

This chapter provides guidance in conducting successful interviews. You should schedule an interview, either on or off campus, at all your target colleges. Be as prepared for your interviews as you are for any important exam. By speaking with an admission officer or alumni interviewer in a one-on-one setting, you have an opportunity to convey who you are and what ignites your passions in an engaging manner. More importantly, you may find an ally in your quest for admission. Also included in this chapter is an interesting sidebar on Waitlists.

Chapter 12: Your Application—Letters of Recommendation

Letters of Recommendation (LORs) present firsthand information about you that's not available elsewhere in your application. They will have a positive effect on admissions if you treat them seriously rather than just items to be checked off your list of things to do.

LORs with your theme embedded within them have the greatest potential to enhance your case for admission, and who writes your recommendations is as important as their content.

This chapter will explain how you should help your recommenders help you. The faculty members who write your LORs need to understand how you want their letters to affect admission officers. LORs should be considered as important as any other factor in admissions.

Chapter 13: Special Populations

This chapter is a guide for applicants who possess characteristics that impose special considerations that must be considered in selecting and applying to colleges. The categories of students included in Special Populations are:

- Hispanic/LatinX Students
- First-Generation Students
- LGBTQ+ Students
- Students with Disabilities
- Undocumented Immigrant Students
- Students from historically underrepresented minorities
- Asian Americans
- International Students

Chapter 14: Resources for Your Research

When you're researching colleges, make sure that you have comprehensive, accurate information about them. There are several categories of resources available for your reference. They're covered in this chapter along with descriptions of them and how they can play a role in your college research. Research resources are categorized as follows:

- Subjective Guides
- Objective Guides
- Magazine Rankings
- The College Cooperative Database
- The Federal Government
- College Websites
- Campus Visits

CHAPTER 1:
HOW TO BEGIN

It's often difficult for a high school student to know how to begin the college admissions phase. As early as fall semester of sophomore year and no later than fall of junior year, you should think about and respond to the questions below. Your answers are likely to change, perhaps many times, as new experiences and changing conditions alter your opinions. Keep in mind that your personal growth is not static. However, this exercise sets a baseline going forward as you leap into the mechanics of admissions.

1. What are your goals for your education?
2. How would you describe your character?
3. What is the lifestyle that you aspire to have in the future?
4. What are your academic strengths and weaknesses?
5. What is the right field of study for you?
6. What are the career prospects in the field of study you are considering?
7. How do you see your future life?

As a parent, you can help by posing these questions and others to your student and then discussing the responses. If your student is reluctant to discuss them with you, encourage him/her to consider and answer the questions privately. Try not to offer answers before your student has had time to consider the questions.

As you endeavor to complete this exercise, consider the following to simplify the process:

1. What are your goals for your education?

If you don't know where you're going, any road will get you there. Understand the goals you seek to achieve and write them down, including any and all modifications you make to them during this journey.

The goals you choose in the beginning are certainly not intended to be fixed and unchangeable—far from it. The whole idea is that you are in a stage of discovery. You're paying attention to any and all information that may affect your decisions. In this mode, you'll have plenty of reasons to make adjustments.

Your personal educational goals are for your reference only. They should be stated briefly and include the information below.

- The career field that is your ultimate goal
- An idea of the kind of college that can best prepare you for this career
- What you need to get into such a college, including:
    - Approximate GPA and rigor of curriculum
    - Extracurricular activities
    - SAT/ACT scores
- The kind of first job you'll need to obtain after graduation to begin your career

2. How would you describe your character?

Many colleges have reformed their admissions practices. They want to convey a powerful new message: admission is partly based on ethical behavior, especially respect for all people and concern for the common good. Colleges look for students who demonstrate these values. They want it known that a student's character is as important to their decision to admit as any other factor.

Character is comprised of attributes—such as honesty, integrity, perseverance, kindness, fair-mindedness, ethics, open-mindedness, empathy, and resilience—that are not easily quantified. However difficult it may be to communicate character, the fact is that it's something colleges will assess in determining if you'll be invited to join their freshman class. For this reason, you should conduct your own evaluation of your character early on so that you will have time to raise it to the caliber that you perceive colleges seek. An added bonus is that you become a better person.

ADDITIONAL CONDITIONAL

Remember that college acceptance is conditional and dependent on the college's ongoing assessment of character, even after admission. Don't risk even the most minor offenses. If you are caught cheating or doing other seemingly "harmless" activities, the consequences will be a lot worse than suspension, detention, or a zero on a test. You will have to report the infraction to the colleges you have applied to before they find out about it from your guidance counselor or another person. Don't assume that it won't happen to you.

In my more than a quarter century of doing this work, it has happened more often than I care to think about, in spite of my advice to my students. It has negatively affected the application results of every one of them. Please, don't be a victim of your own folly. If you think that the colleges may never find out, so you don't need to tell them, think about this: Let's say that you are at the end of your junior year of college, you have done very well and are excited to begin the last leg of your journey. Someone from your past purposely or inadvertently tells your college about what happened in high school. This means that because you did not fully disclose, your application is fraudulent and you began college with a lie. You can be dismissed and lose all that you worked for because of that lie.

3. What is the lifestyle that you aspire to have in the future?
Those students who aspire to the lifestyles of the rich and famous help themselves if they recognize this early. They can then integrate it within their admissions campaign and reflect it in the selection of their major, college, and career. However, you need to contend with two associated concerns. First, a lavish lifestyle isn't always a good thing; and second, it's difficult to achieve. Aiming lower monetarily is more practical and tends to produce a better outcome with respect to personal satisfaction.

You should start by making a preliminary selection of the major, college, and career that seem best suited to you as if money were of no concern. Then, when you're confident that you've made good choices, examine the opportunities within that career field to determine which niches may hold the highest compensation potential. Then aim for one of them. Ideally, you can make all the money you aspire to have while doing something you love.

There are students who are relatively indifferent to compensation. If you're such a student, you're truly free to "Follow your passion!" Take a path that lights your fire. Within reason, you needn't be concerned with the financial benefits that your choice may entail. If your passion lies in the study of the humanities, you're as likely to enjoy a rewarding and well-compensated career as a STEM major.

4. What are your academic strengths and weaknesses?
To the extent that your lifestyle ambitions may hinder your freedom to pursue the fields that interest you the most, an honest self-examination of your own academic strengths and weaknesses is a good idea.

For example, you may want to major in the hot new field of Mechatronics Engineering, which focuses on robotics, because its graduates start at high salaries. But if you hate math and get mediocre grades in it, this isn't a practical option.

On the other hand, you may not see a career as a writer as lucrative, but you've won writing competitions, love to write, and receive excellent grades in English courses. It would behoove you to investigate those niches within the writing profession that promise a level of income that would satisfy your lifestyle aspirations.

5. What is the right field of study for you?

"Follow your passion!" is the conventional wisdom when it comes to choosing a major and career. However, most high school students lack a clear awareness of what career is right for them even as seniors. This is partly because they have not been exposed to the plethora of options that exist. If you're in this situation, we advise you to proceed strategically to select a major based primarily on your interests but tempered somewhat by the viability of the field as a career.

Here's a scenario that exemplifies the challenges in selecting a major. In early junior year, a high school student decided she was interested in pursuing the sciences, particularly the field of medicine. By spring of junior year, however, she began thinking she was more interested in the humanities. Obviously, this was a significant change in direction.

A singular characteristic of this student was that she grew up in several different countries, including ones as disparate as Saudi Arabia and Belgium. For this reason, her guidance counselor suggested International Relations as a major and career. She was enthusiastic about the idea and it took root. As a rising senior, she took a summer course in International Relations at a local college. She also started a global affairs blog and club with friends. Thus, she quickly went from being undecided to having a well-established interest in a specific field of study. She also had a story to tell in her applications, one that encouraged Admission Officers (AOs) to consider her more favorably.

If your near-term goal of a major and long-term goal of a career haven't crystallized by senior year, use your favorite subject as a proxy. Consider this academic field to be your "temporary" major on applications.

Be aware that, when you initially select a major on your application, you're not really committing to it. But describing your suitability for this major and your desire to study it makes you more appealing as an applicant. Admission officers will be better able to view you holistically if you point out your qualifications for a particular major.

Once you're admitted to and attending a college, you can switch majors if you've decided upon one for real. You can do this at freshmen registration or during your first two years, usually without sacrificing earned credits. This gives you ample opportunity to learn about majors that appeal to you more than the temporary one you chose on your application.

6. What are the career prospects in the field of study you are considering?

As noted above, compensation is often the key factor in choosing a career. Therefore, before considering careers, you should refer back to your thoughts about the lifestyle that you aspire to have.

There are many articles online with titles such as "The Ten Hottest Careers Right Now." These are of limited value because you need to know which skills will be in demand several years from now, and nobody has a clue to what they might be. Most of the hottest fields today didn't even exist eight years ago.

It's best to choose a career in the same manner that you select a major—by deciding what interests you and excites your passions. If money isn't a major factor, then stick with this approach. If it is, then your understanding of the field of study you wish to pursue will give you a sound basis for projecting its compensation prospects into the future.

7. How do you see your future life?

Look 10 years down the road. Do you see yourself with a family? Is it important for you to be with them for dinner every night? Is imagining a birthday or holiday where you cannot be physically present to celebrate with your loved ones impossible to even think about? If you answered "yes" to this scenario, then there are careers that you should not consider.

The life of an essential worker (doctor, nurse, firefighter, police officer) means that you will not be at home when you want to be. Someone must be on call on major holidays. Your duty day may fall on your child's birthday or kindergarten graduation. These are things to consider when choosing a career.

Although it is never foolproof, the reality is that certain careers have a more substantial effect on your daily life than others. Only you can decide what is important to you and how you wish to live your life.

CHAPTER 2: AFFORDING COLLEGE

A critical step in your admissions campaign is selecting the "best-fit" colleges to which to apply in senior year. A key factor in "best-fit" selection is cost. You should begin to hold family discussions about finances in late sophomore or early junior year and continue monthly until you've enrolled in a school.

For a generation, the costs of college have risen at a much faster rate than inflation, even though the number of students attending college has declined. This incongruity has become even more acute since the COVID-19 pandemic began, with the volume of applications declining markedly but college tuition costs remaining high or increasing. As long as this situation persists, most families will need to find external sources of funds to help them pay for college.

Although student loans are a ready source of funds for college, this recourse should be considered realistically with an eye toward your ability to pay the debt within a reasonable period of time. Remember that you are part of a family that is interdependent, particularly when considering financial matters. Since one of the most essential steps in the admissions process is how to pay for it all, this usually falls to your parents. Having said that, though, you need to be somewhat realistic in what you expect them to do while still planning for your siblings, if any, and their own retirement. This is the time to candidly discuss with your parents what they believe they can afford to give you toward the cost of college, including tuition, room and board, books, spending money, travel, and all the other items included in the cost of attendance. You should also be prepared to work so that you can contribute as well.

To make ends meet, you, the student, must be prepared to do two things: (1) Search diligently for external sources of funding from the many sources available and (2) adapt your educational goals to fit the available funds. The more successful you are at the first task, the less you'll need to sacrifice in the second. In order to have a handle on the financial aspects of the college process, it is advisable for students to get information about the colleges under consideration. The place to start is by using the Net Price Calculators that every college must make publicly available.

CALCULATING YOUR NEEDS

Parents need to forecast the amount of money that can be diverted from the family budget to pay for college. From this amount, subtract the expense of your child's educational goals. In the great majority of cases, this will be a negative number that represents the amount required from external sources to fill the gap. Obtaining these funds is, for most families, the most vexing issue to resolve.

Parents can determine their financial aid eligibility at FAFSA only schools by using the FAFSA4caster at https://fafsa.ed.gov/spa/fafsa4c/?locale=en_US#/landing.

You can do this at any time, even well before you are ready to begin the college planning process. Once you have this information, you can make more informed decisions about how to structure your financial picture to help your family through the college years. With your estimator in mind, you can then look at the Net Price Calculators for the colleges your student is considering and determine the chances of being able to afford particular schools. Remember that many colleges give substantial merit awards to the students they really want including students who have little or no demonstrated need. When offered to students with need, it typically makes up the gap that the partial need-based offer didn't fill. Few pay sticker price.

1. The FAFSA

The Free Application for Federal Student Aid (FAFSA) is a form completed by prospective and current college students to determine eligibility for federal, state, and certain private sources of financial aid. Your diligence in completing this form is vital to your success in obtaining external funds, both public and private, for your education.

New federal laws were enacted that will affect the FAFSA for the 2024–2025 academic year but some changes will be phased in between now and then. The primary purpose of the FAFSA Simplification Act, signed into law in December 2020, is to make it easier to complete the FAFSA so that a larger percentage of students will submit it to obtain the federal financial aid to which they're entitled. (In 2019, only 60 percent of graduating high school seniors submitted a FAFSA for federal aid, whereas every senior should submit one.)

Revising the FAFSA is a complex undertaking. It will take time to establish new rules and modify administrative processes, so the changes in the act won't go into effect until July 1, 2024, the first day of the 2024–2025 academic year. The new FAFSA form will be available online on October 1, 2023, so students who are now high school sophomores—the college class of 2029—will be the first to use it. For more about the changes, see Table 2A: FAFSA Simplified.

TABLE 2A: FAFSA Simplified

The new FAFSA will be an improvement over the current one in most respects. Changes include a reduction in the number of questions from 108 to 36. Below is a summary of the major changes and what it means for you.

The Income Protection Allowance (IPA) for independent unmarried students and dependent students will increase 35 percent. The amount that student income is protected from consideration has been increased by 35 percent, from $10,840 to $14,630 for independent students and from $6,970 to $9,410 for dependent students. This may reduce the disincentive for students to work toward saving for college.
The term *Expected Family Contribution* (EFC) will be replaced with *Student Aid Index* (SAI). Many parents now mistakenly believe that the EFC is the amount they will have to pay for college, but the real figure is often significantly higher. However, changing the terminology won't help the main problem that parents experience. They don't know the actual amount of the cost of their student's attendance until their child has applied to and been accepted by a college. This is too late to allow for optimal financial preparation.
Federal financial aid eligibility is expanded to and/or barriers reduced. This means that incarcerated students, homeless and foster care youth, and convicted drug offenders are now eligible for federal financial aid.
Calculation of the SAI will change. This will make it easier to identify the neediest students. For example, if a student is eligible for a Pell Grant, the SAI is set to zero. For the first time, the SAI under the new rules can go below zero, which will make it possible to truly see those students with the most financial need.
The amount of the parent Income Protection Allowance (IPA) that is shielded from the SAI will increase. For a three-person family, this will increase by 20 percent.

An itemized Cost of Attendance (COA) must be disclosed on every college's website. COA will include tuition and fees, housing and meals (previously room and board), books and other course materials, transportation, personal expenses, federal loan fees, and any costs associated with obtaining professional licenses, certifications, or credentials.
The current standard, "the parent you lived with more during the past 12 months," for divorced or separated parents will be eliminated. The parent who provides more financial support will be the parent required to report income and assets on the FAFSA. This will close a loophole often used inappropriately by divorced and separated parents.
"Other untaxed income not reported" will be excluded. Such income as worker's compensation and veteran's educational benefits will no longer be reportable as untaxed student income.
"Money received or paid on your behalf" will be excluded. No longer will a distribution from a grandparent-owned 529 account or a cash gift from relatives be reportable as untaxed student income.
The term *Simplified Needs Test* will be replaced with *Applicants Exempt from Asset Reporting.* This will make qualification for aid slightly easier by raising the adjusted gross income cutoff from $50,000 to $60,000.
The law will expand the authority of financial aid administrators to exercise professional judgement. This will allow them to consider a broader range of special circumstances, including natural disasters, national emergencies, recession or economic downturn, and substantial losses in business, investments, and real estate.
Expands the definition of "independent student" This will include students who are unable to contact their parent as well as those for whom contact with their parent would place the student at risk.
The SAI will no longer be divided by the number of family members in college. This change will substantially reduce financial aid eligibility for those families with multiple members in college simultaneously.

The law will prohibit a college admissions or financial aid consultant from charging a fee to help a family in the completion of the FAFSA. This means that families will only be able to obtain FAFSA assistance from volunteers.
The Department of Education and the Internal Revenue Service will more easily be able to share tax data. Student aid applications will be processed faster.

Any student or family in one of the following categories—which includes just about every applicant—should submit a FAFSA: (1) students seeking governmental or private need-based financial aid (2) students anticipating that they may need to seek financial aid at a later point in their undergraduate career (3) families that anticipate having two or more members in college at the same time (this significantly lowers the threshold for need-based eligibility) and (4) students seeking to apply for merit-based aid from institutions or organizations that require the FAFSA.

It's best to answer the FAFSA questions as succinctly as possible. Don't include extraneous information that wasn't requested. Be scrupulously correct. Complete Section G even though some colleges don't require it. It is from Section G that some colleges determine eligibility for merit aid.

The FAFSA bases its determination of financial need on parental tax returns from two years prior to the student's college entrance. This means that the class of 2022 would have the 2020 tax year considered. A good rule of thumb is to think about the tax year that ends in your child's sophomore year of high school. Arrange to have the required family tax returns available through the IRS online link. Also note that half of your child's personal financial assets, such as a savings account in which they've been accumulating money for college, will also be counted among the family's financial assets for FAFSA purposes.

Submit your FAFSA on the earliest possible date. It is released on October 1 of each year, and many types of financial aid are awarded to eligible students on a first-come, first-served basis.

After submitting the FAFSA, you'll be provided with a Student Aid Report (SAR). The SAR provides (1) your eligibility for different types of financial aid (2) Expected Family Contribution (EFC) and (3) a recap of your FAFSA data. An electronic version called the Institutional Student Information Record (ISIR) is immediately sent to the colleges that you have designated on the FAFSA and is also sent to public agencies that award need-based aid. The EFC usually exceeds the amount that your parents think can be prudently diverted from the family budget for college expenses. If this is the case, then there's more work that you need to do to secure additional funding.

2. The CSS Profile

The FAFSA is distinct from the College Scholarship Service Profile (CSS Profile), which is a form required by about 400 private colleges in addition to the FAFSA for financial aid consideration. The CSS Profile is a fee-based product of the College Board. It's a tool used by colleges to distribute their own institutional funding. Check the websites of the colleges to which you'll apply to see if they require the CSS Profile as well as the FAFSA.

3. Private Scholarships

Perhaps you consider College A to be your first choice, but if you were accepted, you wouldn't be able to afford it. A good way to obtain the additional funds is to get a partial scholarship from the college itself to augment your family's budget.

You should be wary, however, when a college, upon accepting you, offers you a partial scholarship. Scholarships are always welcome, but sometimes they're a marketing technique encouraging you to enroll at their college instead of one of their competitors. Sometimes this incentive is not a renewable part of the financial aid package. Be cautious about accepting admission from a college only because it comes with a tuition "discount." If you were accepted by another college in which you prefer to enroll, try to obtain the funding that will enable you to do so.

About $6 billion in private scholarship funding is made available annually to undergraduates. With a dedicated effort, you can improve your chances of winning a share of it. Most high school students apply for college scholarships only during senior year, but you can and should begin the process sooner. Also, your pursuit of scholarships needn't end when you're enrolled in a college. You can continue to seek funding throughout your college career. There are many single-year awards for which students must reapply and recompete annually.

Conduct your search on the internet. There are free scholarship-finding services, such as Cappex, Fastweb, Bigfuture, College Board, Student Scholarship Search, Raise.me, and Unigo. Since there are many thousands of scholarships available, you should let these services do your filtering for you. The time you spend creating an accurate profile on at least two of these sites will be rewarded with results that reflect the most viable scholarship opportunities for you.

Avoid scholarship search services that charge a fee. Applying for a scholarship should always be free. A fee-based service that guarantees that you will obtain a scholarship is certain to be a scam.

You'll need to submit an essay, transcripts, letters of recommendation, and other information to apply for scholarships. This takes time, so begin your effort early to ensure that you submit high-quality scholarship applications by their deadlines.

Below are descriptions of types of or private scholarships to help you focus on those that are the most appropriate for you. Examples are provided for clarity, but they represent only a small part of the scholarships available of each type.

a. **Local Community and Civic Groups:** Take advantage of sources in your community. These organizations seek local applicants for their scholarships, which keeps the pool of competitors relatively low. Many public libraries have a college bulletin board that posts local scholarship opportunities. Parent-Teacher Associations have programs to help fund the education of local students. Identify the local businesses that provide scholarships to area students. They're a common way for business owners to provide a benefit to their community because they reap free positive publicity in return. It's common for service organizations like the Rotary and Lions Clubs, as well as organizations comprised of business owners like the Chamber of Commerce, to sponsor scholarships as a service to the community.

b. **Employers:** Many large corporations operate scholarship programs for the children of employees. If such an opportunity is available to you, you'll be competing against a relatively small set of peers. If you have a part-time job, even as an entry-level employee, you may qualify for a scholarship program through your own employer.

c. **Religious Organizations:** Your religious affiliation may be a source of college funding. Check first with your local place of worship to see if it offers scholarships and then expand your search regionally and nationally.

d. **Extracurricular Activities:** Colleges award scholarships to students whom they have recruited for their exceptional talent in a student activity such as debate or a sport. But even if you haven't been recruited, there are also many scholarships offered by organizations that oversee activities that you may participate in during high school. Activities with national governing bodies are the most likely sources of funding. For example, the Boy Scouts of America offers more than twenty scholarships for Eagle Scouts, the largest being the Mabel and Lawrence S. Cooke Scholarship, which awards $48,000 over four years to one Eagle Scout and $25,000 over four years to four others. Another example is the US Tennis Association, which offers awards such as the $15,000 Marian Wood Baird Scholarship.

e. **Corporate and Philanthropic Awards in Academic Disciplines:** Many scholarships are based on competitions in academic subjects. About half of them are in the humanities—including literature, writing, international affairs, and history—and half are in the STEM fields. STEM employers seek a steady stream of educated professionals to hire, so they underwrite competitions to encourage students to major in STEM fields and go on to STEM careers. Google, Intel, Microsoft, Regeneron, and Toshiba are a few of the corporations that conduct annual competitions with scholarships as awards. Other competitions include the Science Olympiad, International BioGENEius Challenge, Conrad Spirit of Innovation Challenge, American Association of Neuroscience Research Prizes, MIT THINK Scholars Program, Davidson Fellows, and the National Junior Science Symposium.

f. **High Schools:** Some scholarships are available only to students who have been nominated by their high schools. For example, the Morehead-Cain Scholarship at UNC–Chapel Hill offers full merit-based scholarships to nominated in-state students in addition to summer enrichment opportunities. Applicants must undergo a multistep competitive process that begins the summer before senior year. Another scholarship, the Jefferson Scholarship at the University of Virginia, requires students nominated by their Virginia high schools to go through three levels of competition to earn scholarships that pay full tuition plus enrichment activities for four years.

g. **Sweepstakes:** They're certainly long shots, but the easiest scholarships to compete for are those awarded via free online sweepstakes. Simply provide the requested information and answer a few qualifying questions and your application is entered for a chance to win scholarships. Companies such as Sallie Mae, Cappex, and Niche conduct monthly sweepstakes that provide randomly chosen winners with $500, $1,000, or $2,000 scholarships.

h. **Contests:** Essay-writing contests offer scholarships that are less competitive than others because most students don't like writing the essays necessary to compete in them. Some of these competitions have as few as ten contestants. If you're a good writer, you should apply.

i. **Personal Characteristics:** There are special scholarships for those who are the first in their family to attend college. For instance, the majority of scholarship finalists for Questbridge's National College Match program are high achieving, first-generation students from low-income backgrounds. Other private scholarships are based on a student's background or minority status. The Gates Scholarship, for example, offers a number of awards annually to minority students. Through the Looking Glass Scholarships are awarded to students whose parents have disabilities. Children of disabled veterans are eligible for scholarships such as the Military Commander's Scholarship Fund. See Chapter 13: Special Populations for more information on scholarship programs of this type.

4. Federal Grants and Scholarships

There are a number of grant and scholarship programs offered by the federal government that, in the aggregate, award over $100 billion annually. The three largest are:

a. **Pell GRANTS**, which grant up to $6,195 for students whose EFC is low or zero. A 2018 *NerdWallet* study found that students missed out on $2.6 billion in free federal Pell grants by not submitting a FAFSA.
b. **Federal Supplemental Educational Opportunity Grants,** which grant from $100 up to $4,000 for eligible students. Grant money is limited at colleges so it's wise to submit your FAFSA on October 1.
c. **The Federal Work-Study Program,** in which students are given part-time jobs on campus by their college; the Federal government pays half of the wages and the college pays the other half. The money you earn is taxable income.

5. State Grants and Scholarships

If you qualify for a grant or scholarship at the federal level, you may also qualify for one in your state. States operate programs similar to the federal Pell Grant program in that they provide need-based funding that doesn't need to be repaid. If your EFC or SAI is low and your federal financial aid doesn't cover your college costs, state grants or scholarships can provide additional funding.

State-funded grants for minorities promote diversity and increase access to college for traditionally Underrepresented Minorities (URMs). Grant funding is set aside for URMs such as African American, Hispanic, and Native American students. For example,

Wisconsin's Minority Undergraduate Retention Grants disburse funds to second-, third-, and fourth-year URM students.

Specific state funding is also set aside for students whose access to a college education is severely limited by a physical handicap or learning disability. Students contending with other types of exceptional hardship are also considered for specific funding in most states. Those students whose circumstances present the greatest obstacles to education are usually first in line for consideration. In many states, foster care youth are eligible for aid that is earmarked specifically for them.

Students pursuing degrees in high-need fields like nursing, teaching, and STEM may be eligible for special assistance from states. Nursing and teaching grants may be offered in your state in return for an obligation to work in an underserved area upon graduation for a specified period of time, usually two or four years. By committing to work within your state, you'll receive tuition abatement that makes your bachelor's degree tuition-free. You must honor your commitment, or your grant converts to a loan that you must repay with interest.

6. **National Merit Scholarships and the PSAT**

The PSAT is a standardized test administered by the College Board and cosponsored by the National Merit Scholarship Corporation. The test serves a dual purpose: (1) It helps prepare you for the more important SAT exam later in high school and (2) it can make you eligible for the National Merit Scholarship program, which may award you a scholarship to a public institution in your state.

You'll register for and take the PSAT at your high school. The test is composed of two math sections, a critical reading section, and a writing skills section. Two hours and forty-five minutes are allowed for completion of the four sections. The best possible score on the test is 1520.

Taking the PSAT and earning a high score is the essential first step in qualifying for a National Merit Scholarship. To become a finalist, other factors like your GPA and letters of recommendation from teachers are also required, but it all starts with a high score on the test. Less than 1 percent of the students who take the PSAT go on to become National Merit Scholars, but even competing for this honor and being named an Alternate National Merit Scholar is an achievement recognized by colleges.

The PSAT is offered once each year. Only your score on the test that you take in October of your junior year counts for National Merit Scholarship consideration.

7. US Military Grants and Scholarships

The US military pays for college education through its own programs and institutions, including Reserve Officer's Training Corps, National Military Academies, and the G.I. Bill.

a. **Reserve Officer's Training Corps (**ROTC)There are currently over 20,000 cadets in 273 ROTC programs at colleges throughout the United States. The purpose of ROTC is to develop college men and women by training and qualifying them to be commissioned officers in the Army, Navy, Air Force, Marines, and Merchant Marines. ROTC pays for some or all of the college costs of selected students. While the Coast Guard doesn't have an ROTC program, interested students can explore a similar training program, the Coast Guard College Student Pre-Commissioning Initiative.

ROTC students matriculate at a college like any other student. They receive basic military and officer training for their chosen service branch through the ROTC unit at the college. As cadets, they participate in regular drills during the school year and full-time field training for part of the summers. Cadets taking special ROTC classes as part of their curriculum receive credit for them as electives.

ROTC scholarships are based on merit. The primary ROTC scholarship is the four-year program covering tuition, books, and fees. These scholarships are awarded to high school seniors based on a national competition. Each year, more than 4,000 winners are selected from about 25,000 applicants. Depending upon the college attended, a ROTC scholarship can be worth $200,000 or more. Winners also receive a stipend of $1,500 a year and $1,200 annually for books.

During the first two years of college, ROTC cadets have no post-graduate military obligation (except for ROTC scholarship winners). A military obligation begins in junior year if a cadet chooses to enter into a contract with ROTC to become a military officer.

b. **National Service Academies** There are five service academies associated with the Department of Defense: the Military Academy in West Point, NY, the Naval Academy in Annapolis, MD, the Coast Guard Academy in New London, CT, the Merchant Marine Academy in Kings Point, NY, and the Air Force Academy in Colorado Springs, CO.

The admissions processes of the service academies are extensive and highly competitive. All service academies except the Coast Guard require a student to submit an online file and proceed through a pre-candidate qualification procedure before their application is submitted for consideration to an academy.

Admission to the academies differs from other colleges in that applicants must be nominated before they can be considered for admission. Individuals entitled to make nominations include the president and the vice president of the United States, US representatives, and US senators.

The federal government covers tuition and all other expenses for cadets. Upon graduation and the receipt of a bachelor's degree, a cadet is commissioned by Congress as an officer and is obligated to serve a minimum of five years in the military plus another three years in the Reserves.

c. **The G.I. Bill** The Servicemen's Readjustment Act of 1944, commonly known as the G.I. Bill, provided a range of benefits for returning World War II veterans. The original act expired in 1956, but the term *G.I. Bill* is still used to refer to programs designed to assist active members of the US military and veterans to earn a college education.

The G.I. Bill is often used by cash-strapped students to pay for college. In exchange for two years of military service, a student can receive up to $49,248 in tuition assistance from the federal government over a 36-month period. The Forever GI Bill STEM Extension was created to encourage veterans to pursue fields that often require more resources than the 36 months of benefits that are normally allocated. This extension, if granted, will pay veterans up to nine additional months of regular benefits or a maximum lump sum payment of $30,000.

Eligible veterans have 15 years from the date of their honorable discharge to use their benefits if they served prior to 2013. After that date, benefits never expire. Veterans may stop and restart a program as needed. The US Department of Veterans Affairs (VA) administers G.I. Bill programs.

There are two steps in applying for G.I. Bill benefits as a veteran. First, the student selects a college or training program that's eligible to participate under VA rules. Eligible schools are listed on the VA website. Second, the student submits a *VA Form 22-1990* to the VA Regional Processing Office.

Active members of the Army, Navy, Air Force, Marine Corps, Coast Guard Reserve, Army National Guard, and Air National Guard are also eligible for G.I. benefits. Reservists have a minimum service requirement of at least 90 days before they can apply. If accepted, they can serve in the Reserves part-time and go to college part-time. As a part-time Reservist, they train one weekend a month and for two-weeks in the summer. They receive benefits to help pay their college tuition and receive a monthly stipend.

g. **Institutional Financial Aid** This is by far the largest source of aid to students regardless of need. An institutional grant or scholarship is one that's offered to you by a college either after you've applied to or after you've been accepted. Grants and scholarships may be need-based or merit-based. Many institutional grants and scholarships are supported by a college's endowment fund and others are funded by alumni and administered by the college.

Colleges fall into one of two categories regarding admissions decisions and scholarships: need-blind or need-aware. Need-blind schools don't consider a student's ability to pay tuition when making a decision to admit the student. If they admit you, these colleges intend to meet your needs, if any, in the financial aid package that they offer to you. A need-aware college considers your needs when making admissions decisions. Typically, colleges admit a percentage of incoming freshmen on a need-blind basis, then consider the rest of the applicants on a need-aware basis. Students must submit a FAFSA to be eligible for institutional aid. On the form, you can designate the colleges that will receive the Student Aid Report (SAR) derived from your FAFSA. They'll use it to determine your financial needs. You'll also need to submit a CSS Profile to be considered by the 400 or so colleges that require it in addition to the FAFSA.

9. Student Loans

Many college students need loans to pay for at least part of their educational expenses. The two main categories of loans are those that are made under a governmental program and those offered through private lenders. Although federal and state student loans usually have more advantageous terms, you should also consider private loan products.

a. **Federal Student Loans** Submission of the FAFSA is the first step in obtaining a federal loan. There are three loan programs that serve students in different financial situations:
   - **Stafford Loans** are by far the most popular federal loan program. These loans are offered on both a subsidized and unsubsidized basis. Stafford Loans have an annual cap per year, beginning at $5,500 and ending at $7,500. You can use a Stafford Loan to help pay for college regardless of whether or not you have a financial need according to FAFSA. Federal Direct Subsidized Loans have a fixed interest rate that changes by year. The government pays the interest while the student is enrolled in college at least half time. Federal Direct Unsubsidized Loans also have a fixed interest rate for the year borrowed only. If the rate increases the following year, the student pays the higher rate, and interest accumulates in relation to

principal for repayment beginning six months after graduation or sooner if you drop out.

- **Parent Loan for Undergraduate Students (PLUS) Loans** allow students or parents to borrow enough money to fund whatever need is not met by other financial aid programs. They allow you to pay all college costs with almost no money out of pocket. However, your first payment may be due as early as 60 days from the loan's initial disbursement. PLUS Loans are subject to significantly higher interest rates—5.3 percent in March 2021—than Stafford Loans. They are also subject to a loan origination fees of 4.2 percent. They require a good credit history and are less flexible than other types of loans in their repayment options.

b. **Private Student Loans** You may be eligible for loans from private sector lenders regardless of your credit history, grades, or financial need. Private loans can bridge the gap between what you need for college and the total amount of financial aid that you'll receive from other sources.

Federal and state student loans offer the same interest rates and repayment terms to all borrowers. With private student loans, your interest rates and terms can vary because the lenders compete in the marketplace. They are free to create their own loan products as they see fit, although they must abide by the regulations that bear upon private student loans. Your credit record, financial condition, and prospects for repayment, along with a cosigner, will affect the rates and terms of your loan.

There are a great many lenders in the private student loan marketplace. You should research the range of choices before selecting the one that best suits your needs.

TABLE 2B: U.S. News & World Report's Best Private Lenders, 2020

This list does not represent endorsement on the part of the author.

Citizens Bank: Best lender for multi-year approval
College Ave: Best lender that offers only student loans
Discover: Best lender for no application, origination, or late fees
Earnest: Best lender for borrowers with a low FICO credit score
Education Loan Finance: Best lender for referral bonuses
SoFi: Student loan process that's entirely online
MPower Financing: Best lender with no credit history required

Based on the advice of consumer advocacy groups, there are four principal areas on which you should focus when comparing private student loan products: (1) the rate and terms of the loan product (2) your eligibility (3) the total cost of the loan and (4) the value to you of added features.

c. **State Student Loans** State student loans are offered through state agencies or designated state-chartered, nonprofit organizations. The loans are restricted to students who reside in and attend college in the state. State loans have lower interest rates than private loans. They offer the same interest rate to all eligible borrowers regardless of credit scores. Loans have interest rates that, if not based on a specific bond issue, may be reset annually by the state according to the rise or fall of market interest rates. Repayment deferment options may be limited due to restrictions in the state bonds that are the source of funds for the loans.

State loan programs don't operate anywhere near the scale of federal loan programs. Nationally, only a relatively small percentage of undergraduate students receive state loans compared to federal loans. The average state loan amount is $6,400.

Most states offer student loans of some type. These loans are usually reserved for students from the state or those who will attend college there. You can research state student loan programs at GoCollege.com (http://www.gocollege.com/financial-aid/student-loans states).

10. Other Financial Considerations: The American Rescue Plan (ARP) Act

Enacted March 11, 2021, ARP gave colleges resources to implement public health protocols, deploy distance-learning systems, and provide emergency aid to students in need. Three important aspects of the ARP Act as it affects colleges and students are summarized below.

a. **Federal Student Loan Debt Cancellation and Taxes** For years, a much-discussed topic of federal public policy has been the possibility of cancellation, or forgiveness, of federal student loan debt. Part of the discussion has been about whether such debt relief would be subject to taxes as income to students, which would undermine the benefit of loan cancellation to student borrowers and the economy at large. Canceled debt is ordinarily considered income to the debtholder, but this act exempted student borrowers from taxation if their debt was to be canceled. This exemption only lasts until 2026, but it's a key step toward cancellation of some or all of the $1.5 trillion in student loan debt held by 45 million Americans.

   Although it would affect only alumni, loan cancellation legislation should interest prospective applicants who are still in high school because it may portend a future federal policy of tuition subsidization designed to limit student debt *before* it gets burdensome. Such legislative action, as discussed by policy makers, would directly benefit state and community college students and is expected to foster a competitive response that would lower tuition costs at many private colleges.

b. **Assisting States in Restoring Public College Funding** States have cut a combined $1.9 billion in funding for colleges for the fiscal year that ends in June 2021. To make a bad situation worse, tuition revenue has fallen. Enrollment at state colleges declined by 4 percent and enrollment at community college declined by 10 percent in the last year. To absorb state budget cuts and tuition revenue decline simultaneously, public colleges have laid off 304,600 employees. Several public colleges have declared a financial state of emergency and have been forced to close academic programs and lay off tenured faculty. In the upcoming 2022–2023 admissions cycle, prospective applicants should apprise themselves of the impact of pandemic-related budget cuts on the colleges to which they plan to apply.
c. **Change to the 90–10 Rule Affecting For-Profit Colleges** If you are considering attending a for-profit college, you should be aware of the 90–10 rule. This stipulates that colleges are required to obtain at least 10 percent of their tuition revenue from sources other than the federal government. Those colleges not meeting this criterion are barred from being able to receive any of the more than $100 billion the federal government disburses annually in student financial aid. Those that can't meet the threshold may not be such a bargain for you.

SOME COLLEGES WILL FAIL

There are more than 3,500 accredited colleges in the United States, so it's not surprising that a few of them fail from time to time. However, college failures have risen since the turn of the century. A significant number of public colleges have been struggling financially since the great recession of 2007–2010, when state governments reduced educational budgets. Most of these cuts were never restored.

When the pandemic struck, it damaged the financial condition of states, many of which further reduced the budgets of state college systems. Small, second-tier liberal arts colleges throughout the country are also threatened with closure due to the general decline in college applicants. Some colleges have already closed, and others may not survive much longer. Expert observers of trends in US higher education have forecast that about 20 percent of American colleges will close in the next few years due to a combination of tuition revenue shortfalls, changing student demographics, further state disinvestment in higher education, and the inclination of troubled colleges to raise tuition to the point of unaffordability.

Students should research their targeted colleges to assess the likelihood of those schools being among the 80 percent or so that will survive. Even large public and private universities that will survive may tighten their belts substantially despite the injection of cash by the federal government. Stay informed of developments at your target colleges because, even if they're expected to be survivors, they may be forced to close the programs and majors in which you're most interested.

CHAPTER 3: YOUR ACADEMIC RECORD

Your academic record has three components: your Grade Point Average (GPA), your score on either the SAT or the ACT, and sometimes if available, your class rank. All three components are in quantifiable form.

College administrators devise an algorithm that incorporates what they think are the proper weights to assign to factors within your academic record. These include the relative academic reputation of your high school, its curriculum, the courses you chose, and the results achieved—especially in Advanced Placement (AP), International Baccalaureate (IB), and Honors courses. Admissions officers then determine the weight given to your SAT/ACT scores, and, in some cases, your class rank.

Through this algorithm, a college will compute what's known as your Academic Index (AI). Each college determines the point on the index that is high enough for an applicant to be *eligible* for admission. This doesn't mean that everyone above this level will be admitted or that everyone below it will not. It's the core consideration in the holistic profile they'll build for you and all other applicants. So, let's take a closer look at how these components may impact your admission process.

1. GPA

Your GPA is a strong indicator of success in college and is considered more predictive than test scores or class rank. Hence, your GPA is the most important part of your academic record because it measures what you do in the classroom over the course of your high school years. However, the methods of calculating GPA by high schools and colleges isn't standardized. The more aware you are of the variations, the better able you'll be to make the right decisions regarding your curriculum.

It's always been challenging for colleges to compare applicants by their GPAs as if they were comparing apples to apples, which is clearly not the case. First of all, high schools range widely in academic quality. Additionally, there are high schools that have abandoned the 4.0 grading system: Some Texas high schools use a 7.0 scale; others use a 12.0 scale; California high schools submit GPAs that only include sophomore and junior year grades to in-state colleges. Complicating matters further is the fact that many high school teachers now grade less rigorously than was the case in the past. This has moved the bell curve to the right so that students with high GPAs are no longer outliers; they're closer to the mean.

The lack of standardization means there isn't a straightforward method that colleges can use to distinguish the worthy from the unworthy. Nevertheless, grades are the primary factor in admissions, according to the National Association for College Admissions Counseling (NACAC), so how do colleges resolve this dilemma? There are two scales on which GPAs are reported: weighted and unweighted. *Inside Higher Ed* reported a 2017 study that said the average unweighted GPA in the United States was 3.38. This represented an increase from an average of 3.0 reported in 2009 by the National Center for Education Statistics (NCES). We have seen many years of grade inflation as teachers have been pressured to give higher grades for submitted work than the same work would have earned prior to 1980.

When your GPA is reported to a college, the admissions office recalculates it according to its own preferred formula usually taking it down to the unweighted GPA. This is a regular practice at institutions such as the University of Michigan–Ann Arbor, Oberlin College, and many others, as noted on their college websites. A college may choose to include in your GPA only core classes such as English, math, science, social studies, and foreign language, and ignore all electives, except those that fit into the core. For example, taking an extra social studies or English class may be included in the calculation. Many colleges, in an attempt to normalize GPAs, don't consider pluses or minuses that are part of the grades that have been submitted by high schools. And most colleges add points for grades earned in Honors, AP, and IB courses. As such, course selection is very important.

2. High School Course Selection

Beginning early in your high school career, select the right courses to satisfy the requirements of the type of colleges you aspire to attend and for your planned major. The key factor in course selection is the impact on your academic record from the perspective of the admission officers who will ultimately judge your qualifications for admission. They are your audience.

The primary motive to take Advanced Placement (AP) courses is to prove that you're capable of doing college-level work. Another sound reason is to raise your GPA by earning good grades in these rigorous courses. In this respect, AP courses are an excellent means of raising your GPA to a level that truly impresses colleges. About 85 percent of colleges weigh grades in AP courses more heavily than courses in your regular high school curriculum. Many colleges likewise give added weight to good grades earned in IB courses and, if they're known to be equally rigorous, to your high school's Honors classes.

> If you're attending an international high school, it may offer the International Baccalaureate (IB) curriculum. The IB program serves the same purpose as the AP program. It has the potential to demonstrate to admission officers that you've succeeded in an extraordinarily challenging curriculum. IB courses are also offered at many American high schools.

There are now 40 AP courses being offered by the College Board, though few high schools offer all of them and some high schools put limits on the number of AP classes that a student can take. The College Board administers AP final exams in May. If you score a three, four, or five (out of five) on an AP final exam, you may be eligible to receive college credit for that course, depending upon the policies of the college.

AP courses affect your GPA, but not usually in the same way as regular courses. A grade of A in a regular course is weighted as a 4.0 if your high school uses a 4.0 scale, as most do. But high schools will award an additional point for an A grade in an AP course so you can earn a 5.0, raising your GPA commensurately. You can even maintain a 4.0 if you get a B grade in an AP course. In addition, earning a score of four or five on the AP exam may place you above the introductory course in that subject in college, meaning you would have the opportunity to take the next level of the subject rather than the introductory course when you begin college.

A word of advice: Be careful in your course selection to not exceed your ability to produce good results. This is the risk of taking AP courses. They can hurt you as well as help you. Although AP courses can be impressive admissions credentials, they're nullified if you receive poor grades which is usually considered to be anything lower than a B. Avoidance of overly aggressive AP course registration is among the challenges you'll face. For those attending high schools that release class rank and are applying to colleges that require it, consider how to strike a balance between aggressive course selection and higher class rank. If class rank isn't a factor for you, you should take four or five advanced courses if you can do so while producing good grades. A good grade in an AP class is an A or a B, nothing lower. The choice is up to you, of course, as is the decision on which standardized test to take.

3. Standardized Testing: SAT vs. ACT

For several decades, taking the SAT or ACT has been a rite of passage for college-bound students. As a student, you're aware of the strong incentive to perform well on the exams because your score is high among the factors that determine if you'll be admitted to the colleges of your choice. Since all institutions accept both SAT and ACT scores, there's no reason for a college to prefer one to the other. This leaves the choice up to you. To make the decision, assess which exam leans more toward your strengths so that you can attain the highest possible score.

EENY, MEENY, MINY … BOTH?

There are students who take both exams and then submit their best score. This is an aggressive posture, but one that may not be as extreme as it appears. The exams are similar and, for the most part, studying for one is studying for the other, but there are differences in the formats and timing of the tests. Some exceptional students can prepare for both exams without hurting their GPA. The majority of students are advised to stick with one exam.

Before we spell out the differences between them, let's review a few circumstances that may make your test choice easier.

a. **Test-Optional Colleges:** Over 1,500 institutions have adopted test-optional policies, and that number continues to climb, which means you don't need to submit exam scores unless you choose to do so. You should take one of the exams anyway. Then, compare your score to the previous freshman classes of each college that interests you. If your score is above average at some of the schools and it might help you gain admission, then submit your test results to them. Remember that test-optional is not test-blind! Submitting an above-average score will help you gain admittance.
b. **Test-Flexible Colleges:** At test-flexible colleges, such as the University of Rochester (NY), the standard ACT or SAT may be replaced by AP exams of a certain level of difficulty or by another measure.
c. **State Requirements:** There are 21 states (see Table 3A) that require eleventh graders to take the SAT or ACT to assess their academic status. State education administrators observed

that juniors were studying for so many standardized tests that it inhibited their ability to learn their coursework. Since many students were already studying for the SAT or ACT for college admission, the states decided to use them for academic assessment as well. I advise students in states that administer the ACT for assessment to take the ACT again for score improvement if necessary, likewise for students in SAT states. You should be aware that this list is constantly changing.

Table 3A: States Using SAT or ACT for Assessment in Junior Year

SAT	ACT
Colorado	Alabama
Connecticut	Hawaii
Delaware	Kentucky
District of Columbia	Mississippi
Illinois	Montana
Maine	Nebraska
Michigan	Nevada
New Hampshire	North Carolina
Rhode Island	Utah
West Virginia	Wisconsin
	Wyoming

d. **Key Differences Between the SAT and ACT** The best way to compare the exams is to take practice tests. The SAT and ACT organizations make practice tests available online as do many test-prep companies and publications. Compare your results and see if there's a clear winner. In the meantime, here are some noteworthy differences, courtesy of Applerouth Tutoring. Note: As of January 19, 2021, the SAT will no longer have an essay section. The ACT Writing section is optional.

FORMAT AND LENGTH	• 5 sections • Writing & Language; Reading; 2 Math • Total testing time: 2 hours, 10 minutes	• 5 sections • English; Math; Reading; Science; Writing • Total testing time: 3 hours, 35 minutes (includes essay)
SCORING	• Total score: 400–1600 • Evidence-Based Reading & Writing: 200–800 • Math: 200–800	• Composite score: 1–36 (average of 4 test scores) • English: 1–36 • Math: 1–36 • Reading: 1–36 • Science: 1–36 • Writing (not averaged into composite score): 2–12
WRITING & LANGUAGE/ ENGLISH	• Revise and edit a piece of writing • Standard English grammar and usage • Punctuation • Logical structure • Effective rhetoric	• Revise and edit a piece of writing • Standard English grammar and usage • Punctuation • Logical structure • Effective rhetoric
MATH	• Pre-algebra through basic trigonometry 12 Grid-In questions (no answer choices) • Strong emphasis on Algebra • Calculator prohibited on one section	• Pre-algebra through basic trigonometry • Extensive range of concepts tested • Formulas not provided • 5 answer choices per question (rest of test has 4)
READING	• 4 single passages and 1 paired passage • 2 passages include diagrams/charts • 2 vocabulary-in-context questions per passage • 2 evidence questions per passage	• 4 single or paired passages • Consistent order of subject areas: Literary Narrative and Prose Fiction, Social Sciences, Humanities, Natural Sciences

SCIENCE	• The SAT does not have a stand-alone Science section, but 21 science questions are included throughout the Math, Reading, and Writing & Language Tests	• 40 questions distributed over 6 passages • Emphasis on charts, diagrams, etc. • Science is a reasoning test—rarely requires prior specific science knowledge
EXPERIMENTAL QUESTIONS	• Some students receive a 20-minute fifth section after the Math (Calculator) section • Any question from the fifth section or corresponding earlier section may or may not be experimental • All experimental questions test one content area	• Some students receive a 20-minute section after the Science section or experimental questions blended throughout the test • All questions in the fifth section are experimental. • If experimental questions are blended throughout the test, section are extended by 5-10 minutes.
ESSAY	None	• 40 minutes OPTIONAL • Evaluate three perspectives on a contemporary issue • Student opinions encouraged • Scored on 2–12 scale on each of 4 domains: Ideas & Analysis, Development & Support, Organization, Language Use & Conventions

Key Differences:

FORMAT AND LENGTH	The SAT has a stronger emphasis on math, whereas the ACT has a stronger emphasis on science. Overall testing time and section lengths are similar. SAT questions generally require more critical thinking, but the SAT also provides 30–40% more time per question.
SCORING	The ACT Composite score is the average of your four test scores, so a change in one test score may not be reflected in the Composite. The ACT Composite is divided into relatively few possible scores, so an increase of one point can represent a significant difference in abilities. The SAT Total Score is the sum of the test scores.
WRITING & LANGUAGE/ENGLISH	The SAT Writing & Language and ACT English Tests are similar in format and content. The SAT has more emphasis on rhetoric and typically has more complex passages but offers about 33% more time per question than the ACT does. The SAT also includes questions relating to data graphics.
MATH	The SAT and ACT Math Tests cover similar ranges of concepts. The ACT requires a broad, basic knowledge of many concepts. The SAT requires a deep knowledge of a core set of concepts, particularly algebra. The SAT offers about 38% more time per question than the ACT does.
READING	The ACT Reading Test emphasizes basic reading comprehension but challenges students with its speed. The SAT Reading Test emphasizes defining vocabulary in context, understanding the role of the author, and defending answers with textual evidence. The SAT typically contains more complex passages, but offers about 43% more time per question.

SCIENCE	The ACT Science Test measures interpretation, analysis, evaluation, reasoning, and problem-solving skills. The test uses scientific language and reasoning, but rarely requires any specific knowledge from your academic science classes. While there are science questions throughout the SAT, there is no specific Science section.
EXPERIMENTAL QUESTIONS	Experimental questions test the viability of questions that may appear on future tests. They do not count toward a student's official score. On the ACT, they occur in either the fifth section or throughout the test. On the SAT, they may occur in the fifth section or corresponding earlier section.
ESSAY	The ACT Essay emphasizes crafting and comparing arguments. The College Board has removed the Essay section from the SAT.

Adapted with permission from Summit Educational Group's 2021-2022 College Admission Testing Guide.

e. **Comfort-Level Comparison: Take an SAT vs ACT Quiz** Another way you can determine which test is right for you is to take a short quiz provided by PrepScholar.com (https://blog.prepscholar.com/act-vs-sat). In the chart below, check whether you agree or disagree with each statement.

Statement	Agree	Disagree
I struggle with geometry and trigonometry.		
I am good at solving math problems without a calculator.		
Science is not my forte.		
It's easier for me to analyze something than to explain my opinion.		
I normally do well on math tests.		
I can't recall math formulas easily.		
I like coming up with my own answers for math questions.		
Tight time constraints stress me out.		
I can easily find evidence to back up my answers.		
Chronologically arranged questions are easier to follow.		

Now, count up your check marks in each column to find out what your score means.

Mostly Agrees—The SAT is your match!

If you agreed with most or all of the above statements, the SAT is what you've been looking for. With the SAT, you'll have more time for each question and won't need to deal with a pesky science section or a ton of geometry questions.

Mostly Disagrees—The ACT's the one for you!

If you disagreed with most or all of the statements, you'll most likely prefer the ACT over the SAT. On the ACT, you'll never have to come up with your own answers to math problems, and you get to let your opinion shine in your writing.

Equal Agrees and Disagrees—Either test will work!

If you checked "Agree" and "Disagree" an equal number of times, either the ACT or SAT will suit you. Unless you decide to take both, I suggest taking official ACT and SAT practice tests to see which test's format you're ultimately more comfortable with.

f. **What Test Is Submitted Most Often, By State** College Raptor reports that the SAT is submitted most frequently from those on either the East Coast or the West Coast and Texas. The ACT is most often submitted by students in the center of the United States. Because all colleges accept both ACT and SAT and consider them equally, this only tells us the tests that were reported as being submitted to colleges in those geographical areas. The students, though, may be from other states. This trend most likely reflects the genesis of each test. The College Board, which publishes and administers the SAT, is headquartered in New York, New York, and the ACT in Iowa City, Iowa. Both are registered as nonprofit organizations. The College Board's assets were valued at over $1 billion in October of 2020 . The assets of ACT have hovered around $350 million for the last six years in spite of having outstripped the College Board in test administrations for most of those years.

A RANK PROBLEM

About two-thirds of high schools no longer track and report class rank. This has exacerbated the problem that admission officers have in evaluating applicants. To treat applicants fairly, most college administrators now feel that they can no longer use class rank in their decisions because it's not available for everyone.

CHAPTER 4:
YOUR EXTRACURRICULAR ACTIVITIES

The extracurricular activities that you engage in during high school become factors in the admissions decisions of colleges. They are also one of the places in the application that humanizes you. What you choose to spend time on tells a lot about who you are and what you care about. Competition for admission is intense and many applicants are as academically qualified as you are. One of your activities can be the tiebreaker that distinguishes you from your peers and raises you above them in the perception of an Admission Officer (AO).

There are many activities in your school and community from which to choose. It's natural to question which of them might be the most beneficial to an applicant. Unfortunately, there's no set answer to that question. It would be simple if certain activities were clear winners in admissions. But alas, that is not the case.

The most important guideline in your selection of extracurriculars is—more is *not* better, although that was the case many years ago. Now, admission officers look for deep engagement in one or maybe two activities rather than superficial participation in many. Use your application to demonstrate your genuine interest and passion in your primary activity. Don't view this facet of your application as an exercise in spin. AOs develop expertise in distinguishing spin from truth.

ARE YOU *EXTRA* ON SOCIAL MEDIA?

Admission officers will make inferences based on what they learn about you from various sources, including social media platforms and other online activity. Assume they will review your online presence as part of their assessment of you. Your Instagram, Facebook, Twitter, Snapchat, and other social media streams are looked at by most colleges and job recruiters. This is a fact. Your social media, even though it has posts by others, reflects your character and the character of those whom you consider to be friends. If there are those posting things that you or others would find distasteful, get them off your site. Enable as much privacy as you can and take the risk of having fewer "friends." This will help you in the long term.

There are a few activities that high school students intuitively assume will weigh heavily in their favor on applications. These include such things as a varsity sport, a position in student government, or being a member of the drama club, band, orchestra, or debate team. These are great activities, but they're not necessarily home runs. Because colleges want to assemble a diverse student body, they seek applicants with a wide range of talents, skills, and experiences. AOs are as likely to be impressed by a videographer, short-order cook, computer coding club president, homeless shelter cofounder, or restaurant shift manager as they are by a class president or quarterback.

If you contribute thousands of hours to one activity, you'll fare better than an applicant who has a more superficial engagement in four activities. To advance your admissions prospects, commit wholeheartedly to an activity that you truly enjoy, especially if it improves your interpersonal skills and benefits your school or community.

Your activities don't need to be limited to those offered by your high school, although those are usually the most convenient, nor do they need to be a community service activity. A part-time job demonstrates to admission officers that you're practical, responsible, and mature. Unlike volunteering, you must show up for a job, work hard, and perform well. Try to get a job in an area of interest if you can. Even if this is impractical, get a job anyway. Find one that challenges your capabilities and, even better, shows off your potential for leadership. On your applications, state that the wages you earn are to be applied toward college expenses so that you can attend their college. Your case for having sufficiently demonstrated interest for that college will be enhanced.

How to choose extracurricular activities? First and foremost, the activity must be one that interests you. The activities in which you choose to participate are one of three areas that tell the admission officer something about who you are as a person separate from your numbers. What do you like to do with your time outside of the classroom?

- Are you creative, as one of my former students was, and build furniture to sell in your spare time?
- Are you an activist who has created a club to help a population that is less fortunate than you are? I recently had a student who became an ambassador for the education of girls in India, and she developed a club in her high school to raise money for them.
- Years ago, I worked with a young man who designed a method to clean golf balls that he retrieved from the pond at the golf course where he worked. He then resold the cleaned golf balls to golfers for half their cost. He made a lot of money to put toward his college business degree.
- Are you the scientific type? I had a student who had an idea of how to create biofuel. When he was in seventh grade, he began to do research with a local college professor. He continued through his high school years and had his name on the published work.
- Are you a devoted dancer, actor, or singer? The amount of time you spend on your performing art is evidence of your dedication. The roles you have on stage and off are validation of your talent and leadership.
- Do you like to draw or paint? Get out the things you have worked on over the years and photograph them. Write a few

sentences about what the piece means to you and date it. You will then have a portfolio to present with your application whether or not you choose to major in art.

- Have you taken piano lessons since you were three? Make a two-minute tape of the latest piece you are working on with your teacher and put it in your portfolio. When you write about the activity of piano, mention the name of that piece.

There are many ways to show your uniqueness to an admission officer. Make the most of this one. Using your extracurricular activities as an edge in gaining admission to colleges is part of the topic of hooks, which is covered in depth in Chapter 9: Your Application—Theme and Hooks.

DROP THE DAILY COLLEGE CHATS

Parents, try to refrain from making college a daily discussion to the exclusion of all the extracurricular activities and other things your students are doing in their senior year. If you can't control yourself, feel that you will be out of the loop, or fear that your student will not tell you the truth, you should set a time each week where you get to discuss the process and its progress with the student. Make sure that all parties know when that time will be and that nothing interferes with a one-hour block to go through the progress. This should never be at a meal or have siblings present. This is a time for your senior to tell you where in the process s/he is and what is needed from you by way of support. If the student is behind, don't berate. Instead, ask by when the student anticipates catching up to the plan. Then walk away! If your student is not mature enough to get this done on time, maybe it is not the right time for college.

CHAPTER 5: YOUR PERSONAL PREFERENCES

This chapter is a guide to assessing the extent that colleges conform to your preferences. Subjective, nonacademic factors should be the primary influence on your choice of colleges. Subjective factors include such things as weather, distance, campus setting, quality of physical plant, residence halls and dining options, size of student body, student body demographics, average class size, student-to-faculty ratio, mentorships and internships, majors, intramural and varsity athletics, campus social life, science labs, art studios, performing arts venues, and local cultural, entertainment, and recreational opportunities.

Add in any other factors that are important to you, but you should not expect a single institution to fully satisfy all your preferences. We will go into further detail about these factors, but first let's talk about where you should do your research.

1. Sources of Information

The most meaningful feedback will be derived firsthand from your college visits, but there are other sources of reliable information that will help you assess colleges.

a. **College Websites and Course Catalogs** Each college has a website with extensive descriptive content. Many of your questions related to your preferences will be answered by reviewing a school's website. However, be careful to distinguish between facts and marketing because, in addition to their other purposes, college websites are intended to appeal to potential applicants as a recruiting tool. The course catalog will be on the website and usually also available as a download. Be sure to review the catalog closely, especially with respect to the majors, minors, cross-disciplinary programs, and certifications available to students.

b. **Magazine Rankings of Colleges** I advise you not to use magazine rankings of colleges as the key basis for your choice of colleges. The publishers may be well intentioned, but their rankings are based only on quantitative data. Your college choices should be based primarily on *your* subjective criteria. The annual edition of the *U.S. News & World Report of Best Colleges* is the most widely read of the mass-market publications that rank colleges. Rankings based on the same Common Data Set but ordered according to their own proprietary algorithms are published by *Barron's, Forbes, Kiplinger's, Money, Princeton Review, Washington Monthly,* and others.

c. **The College Cooperative Database** Magazine publishers base their rankings on one common data source. It's a shared database called the Common Data Set (CDS). CDS is a collaboration between publishers and colleges to maintain the quality and consistency of reported information. CDS is available for your personal research. To find the CDS data for a college, enter "Common Data Set *Name of College*" into a web search engine.

d. **Federal Government** The College Scorecard is a web-based resource maintained by the US Department of Education for your use in comparing the cost and value of colleges. It provides information in the following categories: programs and degrees, location, size, mission, type of college, and religious affiliation.

e. **Subjective Sources** All of the above are objective sources of information, but subjective analyses are also vital to your research. A good source is the Fiske Guide, which provides reviews of colleges based on feedback from students on topics such as academic programs, majors, intellectual climate, campus facilities, campus social life, accessibility of faculty, intramural and varsity athletics, cultural environment, and transportation. The *Yale Daily News* publishes an *Insider's Guide to Colleges* that is a similar compilation of informed opinions.

2. Preference Categories

The preference categories mentioned above were chosen because they are among the factors commonly cited by students searching for their "best-fit" colleges. Some categories may be of little or no significance to you; ignore them. Focus on the categories that matter to you, add any that aren't listed, and rank the categories in terms of their importance to you. Apply any system of weighting that makes sense to you, e.g., assign a 1, 2, or 3. Then calculate a preference score for your colleges of interest. This will guide you in your selection of the colleges that make your final College List. These are the colleges to which you'll apply in senior year. (Further information can be found in Chapter 7: Your College List.)

a. **Weather:** Weather is a more important factor in a student's satisfaction with college than you might expect. Preferences vary widely. A northern student seeking a warmer climate may prefer to apply to colleges in the Sunbelt. Another student living in the South may aspire to attend one of the excellent small liberal arts colleges in New England and will tolerate the colder winters to do so. Knowing if you have a strong preference along these lines will help you build your College List.

b. **Distance:** This is the distance between your home and your college. There are practical considerations that may impel you to limit this distance. You may need to commute to avoid the cost of room and board. You may prefer to remain close to your friends and families or a job. Cost notwithstanding, young people generally feel that they derive more benefit from college if they live on campus, but the campus doesn't have to be far from home.

c. **Campus Setting:** For some high school students, there's considerable appeal to attending college in a fast-paced urban environment rife with choices in off-campus activities. Others are drawn to a rural setting where the pace is slower, making it easier to focus on studies and socialize with classmates. There are those who seek the best of both worlds by attending college in a small city or suburban environment. Deciding which type of setting appeals to you the most will make the development of your College List that much easier.

d. **Quality of Physical Plant:** This characteristic of a college may not seem important to you unless you're on the campus. How does it look? Are the buildings and facilities new or old? Does it look "college-y"? People tend to have an image of what a college should look like. For some, the buildings should have massive dimensions and feature a combination of castle-like towers, stone walls, spires, pointed arches, gargoyles, and decorative portals. This is American collegiate Gothic architecture, which mimics the architecture of Oxford and Cambridge Universities in England. It became popular in the United States after the Civil War and still conveys seriousness of purpose to people today. Of course, there are stunning campuses in the United States that haven't a trace of collegiate Gothic architecture. Many colleges were built to emulate the neoclassical, Renaissance revival, Spanish, or postmodern styles. If you're a seeker of beauty, add architecture to your preferences.

e. **Residence Halls and Dining Options:** This is an important consideration for many students. Since freshmen are usually required to live on campus, many seek accommodations that afford a certain level of privacy, cleanliness, and convenience. Likewise, the institutional food of yesteryear is unsatisfactory today. Dining facilities are expected to offer healthy and diverse food choices and long hours. Given the changes in the preferences of students, many colleges have invested in upgrades to their residential and dining facilities in order to remain competitive. An appreciation of their quality is best obtained firsthand by visiting campuses. If you cannot arrange to stay overnight in a residence and eat in a dining hall, at least tour the dorms and dining halls and discuss them with students.

f. **Size of Student Body:** The undergraduate populations of American institutions of higher learning range from 275 students at the San Francisco Art Institute to 58,913 at the University of Central Florida, with an average size of 6,365 students. Visiting colleges and getting a firsthand impression of how the number of students affects you is highly recommended. Generally, there's a trade-off. Those seeking a wide-ranging curriculum and extensive campus amenities are more likely to find them at universities with large student populations. Those who prefer smaller populations will find plenty of them but need to recognize that they'll do without some of the big-school amenities.

g. **Student Body Demographics:** There's ample evidence that attending a college with a high degree of diversity in its student population enhances the quality of education. If you prefer to matriculate among classmates who are diverse in race, nationality, age, religion, sexual orientation, and economic status, then research will enable you to identify which colleges offer the highest degree of diversity.

h. **Average Class Size:** Many students consider a small class size to be preferable to a large one because each student receives more individualized attention to facilitate learning. This is the principal reason why small liberal arts colleges are highly valued in academic circles. Other students prefer large classes because they feel that they'll develop better problem-solving skills by being self-reliant.

   A college's average class size may range from five to more than 100 students. Community colleges average 30 students per class. The 90 most highly rated US universities average 38 students per class. Class sizes at liberal arts colleges average 17 students. All American colleges collectively average 32 students per class.

   Of course, the level and type of course in question will affect the size of the class at all colleges. Freshman introductory classes are larger than senior seminars. If you can determine whether you expect to learn better in small or large classes, this will help your College List development.

i. **Student to Faculty Ratio:** The student to faculty ratio starts with the calculation of how many faculty members on a campus are engaged in teaching. The average student to faculty ratio of US colleges is 18:1, according to the National Center for Educational Statistics. This implies that if a school's ratio is above 18:1, it's below average in teaching efficacy. A school with a ratio lower than 18:1 is considered to be above average in teaching efficacy. Since class sizes vary, a college's low student to faculty ratio doesn't necessarily mean you'll never be in classes with a high number of students.

j. **Mentorships and Internships:** Research has shown that there are many benefits in strong faculty mentoring programs. College administrators should foster faculty mentoring programs so that all undergraduates can benefit from them. You should investigate the availability of mentorships programs at your colleges of interest.

Many colleges focus attention on assisting students to obtain their first jobs in their chosen career fields. One of the best ways to gain career-relevant experience is through internships. A college's internship programs should be considered together with other forms of experiential learning, such as research opportunities, fellowships, and externships. You may want to add a visit to the Career office as part of your campus tour to find out how robust their program is.

Each type of experiential learning has different benefits. Intern placements typically last one semester, and students usually receive academic credit for them. Fellowships pay students to participate in scientific research projects. Students interested in such research may be invited to work on projects by a faculty member. Fellowships last for a year and can be renewed depending on certain conditions. In externships, students shadow a professional in the field for a specific period of time.

U.S. News & World Report of Best Colleges considers the following schools to have the most highly developed internship programs among US colleges: Drexel, Cornell, Georgia Tech, MIT, Northeastern, Purdue, Richmond, UPenn, Wake Forest, and William & Mary.

k. **Majors:** It's to your advantage to have a plan to pursue a particular field of study and the career path that flows from it. If you don't have a well-formed plan in high school, which is true of many students, you should still identify an intended major when applying to colleges. Doing so will enable you to present yourself as dedicated to a field of study, which makes a positive impression on admission officers. (When attending a college, you'll be able to change your major if you decide that a different field has greater appeal.) You should check course catalogs to make sure that a degree is offered in your intended major and that the curriculum requirements for that degree suit you. Also note if the college has graduate programs in that major, especially if they're structured in combination with undergraduates in the same major. Majors can be highly fragmented. Although there are many examples, perhaps the most fragmented major of all is engineering. You won't just major in engineering, you'll major in a certain type of engineering. Make sure that the colleges that you apply to offer the specialty that you seek. Table 5A, below, reflects the many different types of engineering.

Table 5A: Engineering Specialties

Aeronautical	Aerospace	Agricultural
Automotive	Bioengineering	Biomedical
Chemical	Civil	Computer
Electrical	Environmental	Genetic
Geotechnical	Hydraulics	Industrial
Management	Manufacturing	Marine
Materials	Mechanical	Metallurgical
Mining	Molecular	Nuclear
Polymer/Fiber	Software	Systems

1. **Intramural and Varsity Athletics:** Unless you're a recruited athlete who is committed to competing in a sport, your interest in varsity athletics pertains mainly to your avidity as a fan. But there are students who aspire to attend a school that has a good reputation in varsity competition, especially in football and basketball. Intramural sports attract the attention of many applicants who wish to participate on a team rather than just root for one.

Information on intramural sports is available on a college's website or elsewhere in its publications. Asking students or alumni is the best way to determine if an intramural program will appeal to you.

> Two related factors that you should investigate are fitness and health. You should determine if the campus fitness facilities meet your needs. The quality and policies of the college's health facilities should also be a topic of concern to you. One thing you must remember to do before leaving for college is to assign to your parents the right to make medical decisions for you in case of an accident or emergency.

m. **Campus Social Life:** Maintaining an active social life in college is beneficial to you in several ways. It improves your study habits, adds to your exposure to new ideas and cultures, helps maintain your emotional stability, builds self-confidence, and helps your career. In selecting colleges, the question isn't whether you're going to have a social life; rather, it is to what extent a college may facilitate your social life. There are numerous publications that release rankings for top party schools each year, but whatever their criteria are, it's best to ignore them. Any college can meet the party criterion if that's what a student wants in a college. Better sources of information regarding a school's support of student social life are the Fiske Guide and the Insider's Guide to Colleges from the Yale Daily News. Both publications provide reviews of colleges based on input from current students regarding, among other things, the overall quality of social life on campus.

n. **Science Labs, Art Studios, Performance Arts Venues, and Academic Support Centers:** Students in certain majors rely on the availability and quality of facilities outside of the classroom to pursue their studies and gain hands-on experience. When researching and visiting a campus, be sure to investigate any that pertain to your intended major.

o. **Local Cultural, Entertainment, and Recreational Opportunities:** The presence of opportunities off campus for cultural activities and entertainment is closely related to your preference for an urban or rural campus. Obviously, an urban setting will afford students easier access to things like sports stadiums, arenas, museums, art galleries, concert halls, international cuisine, and historical sightseeing. Schools off the beaten track often have an advantage in nature-based recreational opportunities, given the greater access to camping, hiking, and similar activities. The expectation of students who prefer small cities and suburbs is that this type of setting will provide the best of both worlds. The types of cultural, entertainment, and recreational opportunities that are important to you should play a role in building your College List.

CHAPTER 6: CAMPUS VISITS

There's no substitute for being there. Nothing you can do will tell you more about a college than a visit to its campus. A well-planned visit will reveal more than its website, course catalog, statistical profile, media articles, and rankings put together. However, a successful college visit requires careful planning, so this chapter provides a protocol to follow that will make your visits more worthwhile. By observing this methodology consistently, you'll be better able to compare colleges as apples to apples.

1. College Visits *Before* and *After*

There are two stages in your college admissions campaign during which you should be visiting colleges. The first is in preparing your College List—the schools to which you'll apply in senior year (see Chapter 7: Your College List). Ideally, your visits should begin in junior year and continue until the early fall of senior year when you need to finalize your applications. It's on this *Before* stage that we focus here.

The *After* stage comes later in senior year. It's brief but important if you've been accepted to more than one college and are unsure which one to attend. Revisit the contending colleges before the decision deadline to compare the contenders head-to-head. Make an overnight visit to your top two options if you can, then decide. Try not to visit on a Thursday or Friday night. Most college students use these two nights to decompress and may give you a false sense of the atmosphere at the college. Earlier in the week is better so that you can attend a class, shadow a student through a typical day and evening and get to know what life is like on campus for most of the week.

2. Planning Visits

Successful college visits require careful planning. We recommend that you employ essentially the same plan for all visits. Doing so will enable you to compare colleges by a common standard.

Research the colleges that interest you using the resources in Chapter 5: Your Personal Preferences. Then search the web for articles about the colleges that interest you. In addition to helping you decide which schools to visit, the knowledge you gain through research will be apparent to the admission officers that interview you when you arrive on campus. They'll appreciate that you are genuinely interested in their school.

3. Activities to Schedule during Visits

Make the time that you spend on campus as productive as possible. Wear comfortable shoes. Take notes and photos because you'll usually tour several colleges in one trip, and they'll tend to blur together. You'll need to make arrangements in advance for the activities below.

a. **Schedule an Interview:** Your first task is to schedule an interview with an admission officer. This requires the most lead time, so make the interview appointment well in advance.
b. **Go on the Guided Tour:** A student-led tour of the campus is a great way to begin a college visit. Schedule it with admissions and let them know if others will be with you. Campus tours usually involve an information session led by an administrator or faculty member. The enthusiasm and attitude of the person giving the information session may tell you a lot about how the college feels about students.

Parents, on the tour and information session, let your student take the lead. Don't push him/her forward or ask a lot of questions yourself. Remember, this is a time to allow your student to form an opinion about the college, so you should not voice your opinions until your student has completed that mental process.

c. **Assess the Classroom Environment:** During the school year, get permission from admissions to sit in on a class that you'd take as a freshman. Even in summer, there are likely to be classes that you can attend to get a feel for the classroom environment.

d. **Experience Campus Life:** Nothing you do will tell you more about a college than staying in a dormitory and eating in a dining hall. If you have a choice, stay with sophomores. They know more about the school than the freshmen, and they're not yet as jaded as upperclassmen. If admissions won't arrange a stay for you, try to make arrangements yourself particularly if you know students at the school.

e. **Learn More about Your Major:** Through the admission office, schedule meetings with a faculty member and a student in your planned major. Use the meetings to ask questions about the curriculum and any special programs within the major. You may want to ask about opportunities for research with a professor or internships that can be arranged for those in your chosen major.

f. **View College Activities:** If you have enough time on campus, attend an event such as a concert, stage performance, or sports competition to get a sense of the campus community.

g. **Follow Your Interests:** Seek permission to take your own tour of facilities that are of particular interest to you, such as athletic facilities, fitness centers, science labs, art studios, and/or rehearsal spaces.

THE DOS AND DON'TS OF CAMPUS VISITS

Always take the campus tour but realize that the student guides are working for the college and are trained in how to respond to questions. Their answers represent the official spin of the college administration. If there are matters that are important to you, investigate them independently and discreetly. Lastly, keep the following in mind:

- Don't ask tour guides what other schools accepted them, what their SAT scores were, or similarly intrusive questions.
- Avoid judging a college based on any one person's opinion or any single fact.
- Keep thoughts about the probability of your admission separate from your impression of the college itself.
- When visiting a campus in summer when the weather is pleasant, remember that it may be much different in winter. Consider whether the campus will appeal to you under winter conditions.

CHAPTER 7: YOUR COLLEGE LIST

Your College List is an indispensable tool for success in college admissions. This is the set of colleges that suit you exceptionally well and to which you'll apply during your senior year. You have laid the foundation for building an effective College List if you've followed the advice in the previous chapters and visited your schools of interest.

> As mentioned in Chapter 6: Campus Visits, students should visit colleges prior to deciding whether to apply to that school and *again* after they have been accepted. Once the preliminary College List is developed, and a visit confirms that the college is as attractive to the student as s/he thought, only then should the student apply to the college.

A key consideration in College List development is the number of schools that should be on it. While there's no "right" number, I advise students to apply to between eight and ten colleges. This is a manageable number and should spread your risk out enough.

Application fees at colleges average between $40 and $90. If these charges are an issue for you, most colleges will waive their fee on request. Some colleges automatically waive the fee for students who have visited or who meet other criteria which change by the year.

1. Set the Requirements for Your List

The first step in building your College List is to establish the criteria against which you'll compare colleges. Choose and prioritize your criteria to suit yourself. Your criteria may include any or all of the preference categories described in Chapter 5: Your Personal Preferences. You should weigh factors according to their importance to you. Most students weigh affordability and academic suitability most heavily.

COLLEGE RANK BY PERSONAL PREFERENCES

Personal Preference	College	College	College	College	College	College	College	College	College	College
Weather										
Distance										
Campus Setting										
Quality of Physical Plant										
Residence Halls & Dining Options										
Size of Student Body										
Student Body Demographics										
Avg. Class Size										
Student to Faculty Ratio										
Mentorships and Internships										
Majors										
Intramural and Varsity Athletics										
Campus Social Life										
Science Labs, Art Studios, Performance Arts Venues										
Cultural, Entertainment, Recreational Opportunities										
Other:										
Other:										
Other:										
Other:										
Other:										
Other:										
TOTAL SCORE										
RANK										

Next, you'll assess how well colleges match your criteria. Start with a preliminary list of the colleges that interest you. Assuming that this is a long list, you need to reduce it through research to a more manageable size. When you've reduced it to about 15 to 20 schools, you can discuss the pros and cons of each of them with guidance counselors, family, friends, students and recent alumni.

The best way to arrive at your final list is to visit all contenders. This may be impractical, so visit nearby schools first to confirm your criteria, then expand outward. The positive or negative vibes you get will enable you to shorten your list. Further details on how to assure the success of your visits to colleges is provided in Chapter 6: Campus Visits.

2. Create Three Tiers of Colleges

A common approach to developing a final College List is to divide the preliminary list of colleges into three tiers: *Likely, Target,* and *Reach.* The tiers are distinguished primarily by their academic requirements for admission. This is referred to as Match which can be defined as where you fall in comparison to the middle 50 percent of GPA and test scores. You'll want to compare your GPA and test scores to the data for a college's freshman class, which is available on their website or from each college's Common Data Set file (see Chapter 5: Your Personal Preferences). The CDS provides substantial detail and breaks down admissions-related data such as freshman GPA and test scores into percentiles so you can see where you stand relative to the most recently admitted students.

a. **Likely (75 percent chance of admission):** A *Likely* school is one at which your academic record falls comfortably above the average GPA and test scores of last year's freshmen. You can feel confident that you'll be admitted to these schools. You should select schools that you'd be happy to attend if your *Target* and *Reach* schools don't admit you, or if you decide not to go to any of the ones that do. You will need to demonstrate as much interest in these colleges as in the others on your list or you may not get in.

b. **Target (50 percent chance of admission):** A *Target* school is one at which your academic record falls at about the average level of last year's freshmen. It's reasonable to anticipate admission to these schools. However, there's an unknown risk inherent in the varying number and quality of applications received from year to year.

c. **Reach (25 percent chance of admission):** Your *Reach* schools are ones that you aspire to attend and at which you have a fair chance of admission. Your academic record places you equal to the lower end of last year's successful applicants, but not so low that you're eliminated from consideration.

> Essays, interviews, letters of recommendation, and extracurricular activities are the best ways to distinguish yourself from other applicants who have similar academic records. Of these, essays have the most potential to help your cause.
>
> As is true with all three tiers, but especially with *Reach* schools, your chances of acceptance are much improved if you possess a strong *hook*; that is, a highly developed talent or skill that enables you to satisfy an existing need that has been identified by a college (see Chapter 9: Your Application—Theme and Hooks).

3. Early Application Programs

The process of identifying the colleges that fit you best and narrowing them down is difficult and time consuming. Adding to the complexity is the need to consider early application programs, including Early Decision (ED), Early Action (EA), Restricted Early Action (REA), and Single-Choice Early Action (SCEA).

Early Action programs vary widely in their terms and options. Your chance of acceptance by many colleges is improved significantly if you apply in the EA cycle but only if you are at the upper end of their middle 50 percent in GPA and test scores. If you choose to apply early to colleges, you'll know if you were accepted before the deadline for submitting applications for the RD cycle. It's important to choose your EA colleges wisely.

Never apply ED unless you fall in the upper end or above the middle 50 percent of GPA and test scores of the college. If you apply ED to a college, you're obligated to enroll and must withdraw other applications you have submitted once you're notified of their binding offer of admission. If you don't do this, they will know, and you may find yourself in the position of having nowhere to go.

The arduous process of constructing an effective College List is worth the effort, since the outcome will be your acceptance at one or more of the colleges that fit you best. It's a significant step toward the accomplishment of your educational goals.

4. Regular Decision (RD) Programs

A college's RD program is the last possible date by which to submit an application. Most are around January 1 but some go as late as March 1. In addition to regular decision, there are many colleges with what is referred to as Rolling Admission (RA). In this process, the applications are reviewed as soon as they arrive and you receive a decision within four to six weeks. Because the class may be filled quite early in the cycle, the sooner you submit an application to a RA college, the more likely you are to be admitted provided that your credentials are in order. It is particularly important that those sending transcripts and recommendations to these colleges are aware of how early you are applying so that they can get it all done in time and are not waiting for your regular decision dates to submit. These schools provide you with a good barometer to determine whether your college list has been constructed properly and has enough depth to it. Additionally, you have the benefit of having a college in your pocket pretty early on in the cycle and this can free you to apply to a couple of reach schools where you may want to be considered.

CHAPTER 8: YOUR APPLICATION—STRATEGY

Due to the competitiveness of admissions, colleges have adopted a holistic approach to the assessment of an applicant's potential fitness to become a member of their student body. In a holistic analysis, admission decisions are based not only on academic qualifications (your numbers) but also on other less tangible factors.

"Stanford admits undergraduates through a holistic review. This means a review of the full set of qualifications and attributes each applicant brings, with a focus on academic excellence, intellectual vitality, extracurricular activity, and personal context."

—E. J. MIRANDA,
STANFORD UNIVERSITY SPOKESPERSON

This chapter is a guide to the development of an admissions strategy that allows you to present your best possible self to colleges. One objective of your strategy is to determine how to distinguish yourself as an applicant. A tool that you'll use to convey your positive attributes is called your *theme*. This is a very brief summary of the reasons why you'll make an outstanding addition to a college's student body. It's to be woven throughout your application package so that Admission Officers (AOs) can't miss it.

You should assess your strengths, accomplishments, and key personality traits in order to make the AO see you as you see yourself.

Then decide which of your unique characteristics you want to stress in the application package. This forms the basis for your rationale as to why the college should accept you rather than the dozens of equally academically qualified students whom they are considering. Once your theme is formulated, you'll be able to enhance your most positive characteristic throughout the remainder of high school. Once you begin to get applications ready for submission, you need to have finalized the theme(s) that you want to reinforce throughout them. You can then convey this information through all parts of your application in a clear and consistent manner.

1. Objective of Your Theme

The objective of your theme is to distinguish yourself from your peers. Most students select nonacademic characteristics to show AOs that they're not just academically qualified but also are distinctive applicants in other respects. The earlier in high school that you identify your distinguishing characteristic, or *hook*, the better the case you'll be able to build in support of it. The hook you go with may be a talent in an extracurricular activity. It may be your extraordinary empathy as demonstrated by your efforts on behalf of the less fortunate in your community. It may be your proven dedication to a particular academic discipline. These are only three of the many ways that you can use a particular characteristic to demonstrate your value and distinctiveness. This is the essence of your personal characteristics that you want the AO to focus on. For more, see Chapter 9: Your Application—Theme and Hooks.

Don't develop different themes for the different colleges to which you apply. Doing so will complicate your ability to make a convincing case. It can result in applications that contain internal contradictions. It makes your theme more difficult to convey. What would you need to do to prove your dedication to X for College A and Y for College B? This approach often gives AOs the impression that the story you're telling is more spin than fact.

Don't try to tailor your theme to each target college. The fact is that all selective and highly selective colleges are looking for the same type: singularly talented applicants who are going to make their individual mark in their own special way. An AO may not know exactly what they're looking for in an individual until they see it on your application conveyed in a compelling way.

The only tailoring you need to be concerned with is your response to the inevitable essay prompt, *Why do you want to go to this college?* This essay will be about how you'll be able to contribute to that particular college. It's not a different strategy for that school; it's the same strategy tailored to demonstrate your interest in attending that school. To write this well you need to truly understand who the college is and how it differs from others like them.

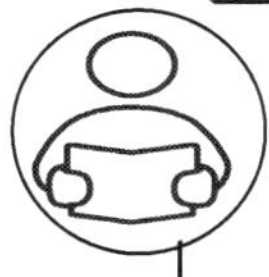

If you are jumping from one application to another, your focus in writing for a particular college will be lost. As you work on each application, keep in mind the elements of that particular college that attracted you to it and work to have those elements present in your writing. This is lost if you are writing for multiple colleges at the same time.

2. Elements of the Strategy

In addition, your strategy should include a tactical plan for the main parts of your college admissions campaign, including:

a. A master calendar that includes the dates of all events and deadlines
b. A plan for SAT/ACT preparation (at least 10 weeks) and scheduling
c. A plan to get optimal letters of recommendation from appropriate faculty
d. A plan for college visits
e. Preparation for interviews by alumni and AOs
f. A plan and schedule for a few well-chosen scholarship applications
g. FAFSA and financial aid applications
h. Your College List

Your strategy isn't a formal document. It doesn't need to be all tidy in a three-ring binder, although this helps some students, it's only important to you. It might be several Word files and a couple of spreadsheets stored where they can be readily accessed. As you grow in self-awareness and maturity, some of the components of your strategy are bound to evolve just as your theme has evolved as you move through high school, but the essence of what you want to convey remains. The changes will reflect the evolution of your personal preferences on things like majors and careers, changes to your financial circumstances, and unforeseen results in test scores or GPA. Events like public health crises and economic recessions can also necessitate extensive changes to your plans. (See Chapter 9: Your Application—Theme and Hooks for more information on this.) Keep your strategy handy and modify it as you choose or need to, so that it's always current.

3. Strategic Considerations

Make use of the technological tools you have to keep track of deadlines. Make a chart or spreadsheet of the application deadlines for each of your chosen colleges. Decide which of the application program options (early, priority, rolling, regular) by which you will apply . Then figure out what types of application are accepted at your colleges of interest. Finally, look at how many supplemental essays, if any, they require. With all this information in front of you, develop a plan of attack.

My students are always finished by Thanksgiving of senior year. All applications are either submitted or ready to be submitted; all the writing has been completed, edited, and finalized. The way to do this is to begin early, usually in the summer prior to senior year, and to work on one application at a time. When the application is finished, submit it, and move to the next on the schedule. An intentional and orderly approach is the only way to not get bogged down by thinking about too many different colleges and their requirements simultaneously. This process may require that your parents nudge you a bit to get things done in a timely manner. Share with them the spreadsheet. Post it on the refrigerator. Do what you need to do to keep your eyes on the prize.

Throughout the admissions campaign, feel free to remind your student of certain facts and deadlines without fear of overstepping. Young people can be somewhat lax regarding deadlines, and that's a costly mistake in the context of admissions. A missed deadline indicates a more serious problem. If the student is behind, don't berate. Instead, ask when the student anticipates catching up to the plan. Then walk away! If your student is not mature enough to get this done on time, maybe it is not the right time for college. An educational consultant can be a great help with procrastinating students.

The following four chapters focus on the other aspects—themes and hooks, essays, interviews, and letters of recommendation—of your application package.

CHAPTER 9: YOUR APPLICATION—THEME AND HOOKS

The authenticity of the distinctive characteristic (your theme) that makes you stand out is vital to your essays and personal statements. To make it more effective, your true story should also be subtly woven into your college interviews and letters of recommendation.

There can be many different types of themes, but what they all have in common is that they *show* who you are at your center. Are you a person who is devoted to your family, your religious institution, your charity? Do you go out of your way to always help other people regardless of whether you know them well or not at all? Have you had a job since your early teens and value the lessons you have learned from hard work? Do your bosses tell you how much you add to the business because of the way you are able to handle difficult customers?

Maybe none of these ring true for you, but you have shown tremendous intellectual curiosity since you were a small child. Are you that kid who can't let a topic go until you have ferreted out the answer even if that means you spend countless hours digging into the topic and reaching out to teachers, reading books, or doing research to find the answer? Are you so fascinated by computers that you have been taking them apart and putting them back together since you first were presented with one?

Only you can determine what facet of YOU it is that you want the college to focus on. Then you need to weave that message about yourself throughout your application. The caveat is that this must be something that is true and ever-present. If you try to fit your history to a theme that sounds great but is not really you, your whole application will ring false. Think about what is important to you not what you or someone else thinks will look good on a college application. Admission Officers (AOs) read thousands of applications. Many of them may have a similar message but it is only by pointing to *your* personal history that you can illustrate the truth of yours. Don't worry about seeming corny or soft. If one of the joys of your life has been helping the old couple down the street with their yard work and doing errands for them in exchange for listening to their stories of the history that they lived through, you are a caring person who has a love for living history. Either of these can be your theme. You may even be able to weave them both into your application.

My point is that we are each unique. There is something about you that makes the world a more interesting place even if that is only for yourself. I once had a student who was the quintessential STEM student. He had spent his summers doing research in a lab with a professor from the local college since he started high school. He was committed to all things scientific. This was his obvious theme, but in getting to know him, I discovered that he was a master pianist. No one knew this about him because he kept it to himself. He used music and the piano to calm himself, to help him think. Now, there are many instances of scientists loving music, but in this instance the first time that he recognized the connection between music and his scientific mind was when he was writing his essay. This opened him to seeing that science was not his only talent, and he began to see himself as a more complete person. The connections in his life became clear and his theme was one of a multi-faceted person who loved to conquer challenges whether they be in the lab, at the piano, or in his interactions with his peers where he was best known for his ability to de-escalate difficult situations because he could see them so clearly.

You have some element of yourself that makes you proud or that you have worked hard to develop. You may have done this without realizing it, but now see it as the essence of you. Dig deep. Find it, and that is your theme. You may want to ask your best friend or most trusted teacher how you are seen by them. What others see in us is often a better measure of who we are than what we think of ourselves.

Hooks

If you're exceptionally talented in, say, a performing art or a sport, then you may have what's referred to in the college admissions field as a *hook*. A hook adds to your appeal as an applicant beyond what you can expect from your academic record and the soft factors described in other chapters. Your hook, if managed and communicated effectively, can help you gain admission to a college that otherwise *wouldn't* accept you. In addition to securing admission, a strong hook can also benefit you by generating scholarship offers.

There are many seats in freshman classes, especially in private colleges, that are awarded to applicants based at least partially on their hook. These applicants may be the legacy children of alumni or have a talent that's highly valued in a collegiate activity or academic discipline. Successful hook applicants can comprise between 25 percent and 50 percent of the freshman class in a private institution. These students are *not* admitted solely on the criteria applied to the general applicant pool. There may not be an academic slacker among them, but their qualifications aren't better than those of all rejected applicants.

It helps to understand why colleges prefer applicants with strong hooks in the form of exceptional talents and skills. They do so because these students are more likely to graduate and achieve distinction and renown in the professional world. This will reflect positively on their alma maters. The more its graduates achieve, the better a college's reputation becomes. The better its reputation, the more students will apply and the more highly qualified those students will be. (The thinking is, if students are applying because of the achievements of former students, they are likely to be achievers as well.) The more students apply, the greater the school's flexibility in raising tuition. It's a "win-win" positive reinforcement cycle for a college.

The renown of its graduates also increases a college's fundraising capacity. College trustees and administrators seek to add to endowment funds as much as possible. So, except for the few applicants whose hooks focus on achieving socioeconomic diversity, hooks have value to a college for financial reasons. Therefore, to use a hook to get into a top-tier college, you should strive to demonstrate your potential to succeed in the future by achieving noteworthy success in high school.

> As a parent, you can help your child develop a talent into a successful hook. However, doing so almost always obligates you and your student to begin early in high school or sooner. We've all heard stories of parents driving their child to practice or lessons at all hours, year-round, for many years. This is the type of commitment usually required to develop a strong hook based on a student's talent, skill, or outstanding ability in an academic field.

1. Legacies

A legacy applicant is one whose parents, grandparents, and/or siblings received their undergraduate degree from the institution to which the student is applying. Graduate or professional degrees do not count as legacy. The student needn't take any action to make use of this status as a hook.

Although endowing legacy status with an advantage in admissions is a practice that draws criticism, many colleges continue to favor it. In the highly competitive college admissions environment, a student shouldn't hesitate to take advantage of their standing as a legacy if they wish to attend a family member's alma mater.

Administrators and trustees at private institutions can be expected to support legacy preferences. They value tradition, so they create and maintain lasting bonds with families. The benefits to a school's fundraising performance that are sustained by legacy policies are vital to that school's financial condition.

Being a legacy doesn't assure you of admission, but it helps. Legacy students usually have good academic records. Admission officers aren't tempted to dip down on the Academic Index (AI) to reach a legacy who has a mediocre academic record. Most legacies score high on the AI. Even so, top-tier private institutions accept only about one-third of the legacies who apply to them due to the intensity of the competition. However, one-third of legacy applicants can still translate to over 25 percent of freshmen at some colleges. As such, there is long-standing opposition to legacy admissions policies.

> *"The easiest way for elite universities to bridge the growing economic divide on their campuses and have their student bodies look like the rest of America is to eliminate legacy admissions."*
>
> —JEFFREY SELINGO IN THE WASHINGTON POST

Pro-legacy observers note that eliminating legacy admissions would have little effect on the socioeconomic diversity of a college's student body. Unfortunately, this may be true because a student's test scores and GPA closely correlate with her/his socioeconomic status. The highest hurdle for disadvantaged students in gaining admission to elite institutions is their relatively weak academic qualifications compared to those of, say, the children of Stanford or MIT graduates. Because they're usually more affluent and have greater educational advantages, the latter tend to have better academic records than the former, so they're better qualified as applicants. The problem, and it is a severe one, is more a factor of the socioeconomic imbalances in our society than in the inherent unfairness of legacy admissions.

> If you're an alumni parent, I recommend that your son or daughter leverage the legacy status to improve their chances of admission to your alma mater. Your post-graduate involvement with the college will also be considered, including donations, participation on boards and committees, assisting in fundraising events, and service in roles such as alumni interviewer provided that these activities did not begin when your student entered high school. The college will assume that you will stop giving as soon as your student is accepted.

If you're applying as a legacy student, declare this on your application by identifying all family members who are alumni. On most applications, including the Common App, there's a section for the description of the educational background of parents. Legacies can also develop other hooks that will make them more appealing to schools on their College List other than their parent's alma mater.

2. Identifying and Using Your Hook

There's a wide range of talents and skills that you may have that can be developed into effective hooks. Identifying a potential hook is a key part of the formulation of your admissions strategy (see Chapter 8: Your Application—Strategy). One objective of your strategy is to determine how to distinguish yourself as an applicant. Decide on the characteristic or theme that will enable you to make the case that you're not just academically qualified and have done well on the soft factors of admission, but that you're also an extraordinary individual who would be a great addition to a college's freshman class.

The earlier in high school that you identify your hook, the better the case you'll be able to build in support of it. Some examples of the characteristic that you might choose are listed below:

- Talent in an extracurricular activity such as a sport, art, or debate
- Leadership skills and applied knowledge developed as an employee
- Extraordinary compassion as evinced by your volunteer efforts, especially in a leadership role
- Experiences while living in a foreign or exotic locale such as, for example, the north slope of Alaska, the Amazon rain forest, or a Middle East war zone
- Experiences as an underrepresented minority student
- Life experiences under difficult circumstances or severe hardship
- Exceptional proficiency in and dedication to a specific academic discipline

These are but a few of the characteristics that you can develop to demonstrate your value and distinctiveness to colleges. The key word is *develop*. Even if your hook arises from a natural gift, you should start early to develop it further through hard work and dedication. Remember that the answer to the age-old question, "How do I get to Carnegie Hall?" is still "Practice!"

3. Honing and Communicating Your Hook

You need to build a case for your hook and communicate it to colleges. Apply the maxim, "If you've got it ... flaunt it!" With the exception of renowned athletes who are recruited by colleges, colleges won't find you unless you make them aware of who you are, what you've done, and what you can do.

Below—as an example of the way applicants can focus attention on their hook—is a message development procedure for athletes.

a. **Using Sports as a Hook:** Athletes should develop a sports résumé—a summary of your accomplishments in a sport that will be included in your application package and submitted to coaches. If you have developed websites or social media pages that include your résumé information and videos that highlight your achievements, you should provide links to them on your résumé. Sports résumés should include:

- **Personal Information:** Name, address, email, phone, and name and address of high school
- **Academic Record:** In addition to test scores and GPA, add related information that won't be reflected in your AI score, such as honors, awards, AP/IB/Honors courses, and class rank.
- **Sport Involvement:** List your teams and their records, describe the leagues in which you competed, positions played, status as starter or reserve in different years, leadership roles, and awards.
- **Performance Statistics:** These are best displayed in tabular or graphic form with explanatory notes.
- **Testimonials from Coaches:** These may be excerpts from letters of recommendations (LORs). You should obtain LORs from coaches, athletic directors, and others considered to be knowledgeable by college coaches.

Athletes should also prepare by learning the recruiting rules of the NCAA and leagues of the relevant college sports teams. Lastly, coaches don't have the bandwidth to communicate at length with non-recruited athletes, so plan your limited opportunities carefully.

There are many types of athletic endeavors that don't involve a major sport but that can still serve as a hook, such as competitive kayaking, mountain climbing, waterskiing, skateboarding, and hang gliding.

b. **Other Performance-Based Hooks:** Students with any hook that involves being assessed against a performance standard should use a variation on the methodology above to communicate their hook to the head of the appropriate department. This includes music, acting, dance, voice, and debate, among other talents. Artists and performers should create a portfolio that attractively presents the best samples of their work.

Although the methodology recommended for performing artists and athletes are similar, athletes are given higher priority in admissions than the arts. Varsity coaches, especially in major sports, exert great influence when they give the admission office the list of athletes that they're recruiting. This list is usually honored as long as the athletes have high enough AIs to be admitted. Unfortunately, outstanding musicians, visual artists, actors, singers, and dancers shouldn't expect the same treatment as athletes. Big-time sports are huge moneymakers for many colleges, including those in the Ivy League, that don't use scholarships to recruit athletes.

4. Using Competitive Awards to Build Your Case

Successful participation in prestigious competitions is a key consideration for students whose hook is extraordinary proficiency in an academic field. Using these competitions to establish the credibility of your hook can be effective in both the STEM fields and the humanities. Success in such competitions brings recognition that helps you make your case. In addition, competitions often award substantial cash prizes or scholarships to winners and finalists.

The Common App has a section that specifically asks you to list any awards or honors that you received during high school. Leaving it blank won't necessarily hurt your chances, but it certainly doesn't help. Citing a well-known competitive award that you've received makes you stand out. The more prestigious the competition and the higher your level of success—school, region, state, national, or international—the greater the impression made on an AO.

About half of student competitions are in the humanities, including literature, writing, international affairs, and history. The other half are in the STEM fields. Majoring in a STEM subject can lead to a career in a fast-growing job category. Since STEM employers have many professional jobs to fill, they use competitions to encourage students to major in their fields.

The list below includes competitions designed to motivate students to think critically and creatively in different academic fields.

a. **American Association of Neurosurgeons (AAN) Prize:** Students investigating problems concerning the brain and nervous system are invited to compete for monetary prizes and trips to the AAN annual meeting to present their work.

b. **Conrad Spirit of Innovation Challenge:** Participants work in teams to develop solutions to some of the world's most pressing and complex problems. Finalist teams compete for college scholarships.

c. **Davidson Fellows:** This prestigious scholarship awards up to $50,000 annually to students who have submitted a significant work in one of eight categories: engineering, mathematics, science, literature, music, technology, philosophy, and "outside the box."

d. **eCYBERMISSION:** Sponsored by the US Army, this is a STEM competition open to teams of high school students who compete for state, regional, and national awards. Teams propose a solution to a given real-world problem. Prizes of $5,000 are awarded to winning team members.

e. **ExploraVision:** Jointly sponsored by Toshiba and the National Science Teachers Association, ExploraVision encourages collaboration by considering only group projects. Participants win gifts and the top four teams receive $10,000 per student.

f. **First Tech Challenge:** This competition involves teams of ten members from the same school who design, build, program, and operate robots. The contest has one top prize plus awards in categories such as motivation and inspiration.
g. **Google Science Fair:** Beginning with online submissions, this competition invites young scientists from around the world to compete for up to $50,000 in scholarships as well as a trip to the Galapagos Islands sponsored by National Geographic. Finalists are invited to Google headquarters, all expenses paid, to present their projects before expert judges.
h. **Intel International Science and Engineering Fair:** Intel hosts the world's-largest international precollege science competition, with 1,800 students selected from all over the world to compete for $4 million in awards. The competition culminates in the fair, which is held annually in different cities.
i. **International BioGENEius Challenge:** This competition is designed to recognize outstanding research in biotechnology among high school students. Finalists showcase their research before a panel of biotech experts. Participants have the opportunity to win substantial cash and scholarship awards.
j. **International Public Policy Forum:** This is an international contest open to high school teams that compete for awards and scholarships. The initial requirement is to submit a team's qualifying essay. From these, the top 64 teams are selected. They begin a single-elimination written debate tournament until the final eight teams are chosen. Expenses are paid for these teams to go to the finals in New York. They then compete in oral debates before a panel of judges that includes experts in law, business, politics, and debate.
k. **Microsoft Imagine Cup:** This is a global competition for students who plan to major in computer science. Teams use their creativity, passion, and knowledge of technology to compete for cash awards, travel, and other prizes.

l. **MIT THINK Scholars Program:** The THINK Scholars program is an initiative that promotes STEM subjects by funding projects developed by high school students. Finalists receive paid trips to MIT to attend its Annual Tech Symposium. Winners receive scholarships and $1,000 to execute their projects.

m. **National History Day Contest:** This is a nonprofit educational organization with a focus on historical research and interpretation. Their largest academic program is the National History Day Contest in which more than half a million students compete each year. Students choose a historical topic related to the annual theme, and then conduct primary and secondary research. After analyzing their research results, students draw a conclusion. Work is submitted in a paper, exhibit, performance, website, or documentary format. Student projects are entered into competitions in the spring. At the first two levels, local and regional, professionals in historical research evaluate the projects, with the best entries advancing to the national finals in June at the University of Maryland.

n. **National Junior Science and Humanities Symposium:** Students compete for scholarships by presenting the results of their original research before a panel of experts and peers. Scholarships as well as eight prizes of $12,000 are awarded to national finalists.

o. **Regeneron Science Talent Search:** This competition invites high school scientists to present original research to a panel of nationally recognized scientists. Forty finalists are selected to come to Washington, DC, to compete for the top award of $250,000.

p. **Scholastic Art & Writing Awards:** This program awards scholarships to high school students in 29 categories, including sculpture, architecture, painting, photography, poetry, dramatic scriptwriting, fashion, animation, and video games. The program was founded as a writing competition to recognize artistic and literary talent, but over time grew to include the current broad range of categories. A few past winners have been Andy Warhol, Sylvia Plath, Truman Capote, Stephen King, John Updike, Lena Dunham, and Joyce Carol Oates.

q. **Science Olympiad:** One of the better-known STEM competitions, this is a contest in which teams of 15 students compete in 23 events in various categories such as anatomy and physiology, tower building, rocks and minerals, and forensics. Substantial cash prizes and scholarships are awarded to members of the winning teams.

r. **US Presidential Scholars Program:** This program recognizes students who excel in the visual, creative, and performing arts as well as in technical subjects. Presidential Scholar awards are considered one of the nation's highest honors. Seniors who have scored exceptionally well on the SAT or ACT are eligible. If invited, students submit essays, transcripts, and self-assessments that are evaluated on academic achievement, personal characteristics, leadership, service activities, and the quality of submitted writing. In April, the Commission on Presidential Scholars selects 121 winners.

CHAPTER 10: YOUR APPLICATION—ESSAYS

The quality of your essays may be the difference between your acceptance or rejection. Essays are the most important of the soft factors that influence college admissions decisions.

As mentioned previously, you should identify your distinctive characteristics early in high school. These characteristics complement your talents, interests, and experiences to make you an attractive addition to a college's population. You must, however, assure that Admission Officers (AOs) get this message loud and clear so that they'll see you as more worthy than your academic peers. The best way to do this is through a carefully crafted, compelling essay that clearly illustrates your theme. Show don't tell! If you can make a positive, gut-level connection with the AO, your essay is a success.

1. Writing Outstanding Essays

Nothing inspires more fear and trepidation in admissions than essays, so it's natural for you to wonder how your essays will be evaluated. You may be apprehensive because you consider yourself only an average writer. The number of essays, short-answer questions, and personal statements that you're required to write may intimidate you. If these are your concerns, you can relax.

Upon receiving your application, colleges compute your Academic Index, or AI, as noted in Chapter 3: Your Academic Record. Once it has been established that your score on the AI is sufficiently high to make you eligible for admission, the job of an AO is to seek reasons to admit you, not reject you.

AOs want to learn more about you through your essays. Of course, they'll also be seeking evidence of your intelligence, but they mainly want to discover things about you. They want to get an idea of how well you'll fit in at their school. They want to get to know the person behind the numbers.

Essays are evaluated from different perspectives. AOs want to know how well you write because writing is considered an important skill no matter what major you choose. Your writing ability will be assessed by the persuasiveness and structure of the story you're telling. On a deeper level, your essay will be weighed by the positive information it uncovers about your maturity, character, personality, and dedication.

Your understanding of the particular colleges to which you're applying is important in the personal statement on the Common Application or in your answer to the essay prompt, *Why do you want to go to our college*? In these, you should demonstrate how you'll contribute to that college. In other essays, especially the supplements, you shouldn't try to discern what that college wants to see and then tailor your essay accordingly. This will lead to problems and may even lead to the admission officer's perception that the essay is inauthentic, which is the kiss of death in the evaluations of essays.

The basis of an outstanding essay is to write in a way that explains who you are. If the essay ties into your passions, it will come alive for the AO. Tell a unique, moving story authentically and succinctly. The great majority of AOs are alumni only a few years older than you.

Students have the right to autonomy in the writing process. Try not to criticize what your student has written. And never write for your student. This is easily discernible by colleges and tells your student that you do not have confidence in his/her ability to be accepted without your intervention.

2. Copy Editors, Not Coauthors

You're on your honor to write essays without assistance from any other person. Even if you succumb to temptation and forego your honor, AOs are experts in discerning the authorship of essays, so don't try it. You may, however, accept the assistance of other people in the brainstorming sessions that precede your writing to help identify the topic that you'll write about. Once this is determined, you'll be writing a first draft of the essay on your own.

You *are* allowed to use the services of an editor. Let me be clear: What I mean by an editor is a *copy editor.* Copy editing is the process of revising written material to improve its readability and fitness for its purpose. It ensures that the writing is free of grammatical and vocabulary errors. The best writer in the world, whoever s/he may be, needs and most likely uses the services of a copy editor. The kind of editor that you cannot use is one who would examine your execution of the topic and make or recommend major modifications to it. Only copy editing is allowed!

Though it's unethical, some students ask a favorite English teacher to assist with their essays. If the teacher consents, you can be confident that your grammar and vocabulary will be correct. The downside is that your essays are less likely to appeal to AOs, who expect essays to be intriguing, conversational, entertaining, and persuasive rather than erudite.

There's a term that describes writing that is meant to be intriguing, entertaining and persuasive—*marketing copy.* Marketing is the act of selling a product, service, idea, or, in this case, yourself.

English teachers are unlikely to be familiar with marketing writing because it has different rules. There *are* rules for writing marketing copy, but they're not the same rules that English teachers value. Marketing allows you to write less-than-perfect sentences in the interest of being intriguing, entertaining, and persuasive—as long as the AO *gets it.*

In a college essay, the marketing message must be subtle. It's not as bold and ingenuous as the "ad-speak" exemplified by "*Nobody doesn't like Sara Lee*!" It's okay to sin against orthodoxy to make a point or express an idea. When you write in the vernacular—the way people speak—your message is more readily understood. Hence, the AO has a few extra seconds to absorb it.

Many English teachers are talented writers, but few have the savvy to advise you on essays. Your essays need to appeal to AOs twice over.

First, you grab their attention with your writing style. Then, your true story motivates them to advocate for your acceptance.

3. Supplemental Essays

Many students are encouraged to focus primarily on their main essay in the Common Application, so supplemental essays are sometimes neglected. Yet, supplemental essays are vital to admission to the colleges that require them.

Let's consider a typical prompt for a supplemental essay: *Please elaborate on one of your extracurricular activities or work experiences.*

If you have developed a strategy, essays are the best opportunity to put it into action. You've invested time and effort to build a case for a distinctive characteristic that you possess. Your case can be proven by relating your experiences in a job, pastime, extracurricular activity, area of interest, or a combination of things. Try to convey your passion as well as your skills, leadership capabilities, and personal initiative. It is also okay to reveal your insecurities as long as you also show how you deal with them in a positive and productive way.

If you're a senior preparing to apply to colleges, but you haven't yet developed a theme, then do the best you can to make up for lost time. If you can take a positive characteristic and fit your experiences to it retrospectively, then do so. You'll need to emphasize relevant aspects of your high school career, but don't fabricate facts to suit your purpose.

The limit on supplemental essays varies between 200 and 650 words. You'll want to overwrite your essay and then pare it back by deleting the least important points. Then restructure it within the specified word limit. Don't exceed the limit. Frankly, I believe that a main essay that runs between 450 and 550 words is ideal. Those who are reading your essay are usually overworked in the reading season and if you don't grab their attention in the first paragraph or two, they may not read the whole thing.

Many colleges require the submission of one or more supplemental essays that respond to their own set of prompts. However, there are many highly regarded colleges that don't require additional essays and rely solely on the Common App essay. You should consider applying only to institutions in this category if you want to avoid writing more than one essay or if, for whatever reason, you're too close to the application deadline to do justice to any supplemental essays that may be required. I must add that this is not a good reason to choose a college.

> Try not to nag, but also make sure your student knows s/he must respect your parental right to ask questions. Reinforce this fact calmly and softly.

CHAPTER 11: YOUR APPLICATION—INTERVIEWS

Although not required by many colleges, most colleges will consider interviews to be a factor in admission. By speaking with you in a one-on-one setting, an admission officer or alumni interviewer has an opportunity to learn about you and what ignites your passions and interests. Schedule an interview at all colleges on your College List, if possible. You should be as well prepared for your interviews as you are for an exam.

Some colleges conduct interviews only to try to recruit you as an applicant. These are informational interviews and they don't consider them in admission decisions. The other type of interview is the evaluative interview in which your suitability for the school is being judged. The majority of the colleges that conduct interviews, whether informational or evaluative, factor them into the decision in some way. This is especially true of colleges that track and score the *demonstrated interest* of applicants. Read the admissions section of a college's website to determine the role that interviews play in their process.

1. The Importance of Interviews at Different Colleges

Research by the National Association for College Admissions Counseling (NACAC) shows that interviews are given different weights by colleges. A survey conducted in 2017 showed that 5.5 percent of colleges afforded considerable importance to interviews, 16.4 percent afforded moderate importance, 28.3 percent afforded some importance, and 49.8 percent assigned little or no importance to interviews. Private colleges and smaller colleges placed relatively more importance on the interview, NACAC found in its *2019 State of College Admission* report.

Many of the most selective institutions require an interview or recommend one; see Table 11A.

Table 11A: Highly Selective Colleges that Require or Recommend an Interview

College	Interview Policy	Interview Purpose
Bowdoin College	Recommended	Evaluative
Brown	Recommended to submit video portfolio	Evaluative
Columbia	Recommended	Evaluative
Connecticut College	Recommended	Evaluative
Cornell	Required for Architecture program and the School of Hotel Administration, recommended for the Art program	Informational
Dartmouth	Recommended	Evaluative
Duke	Recommended	Evaluative
Georgetown University	Required	Evaluative
Hamilton College	Strongly recommended	Evaluative
Harvard	Recommended	Evaluative
Haverford College	Recommended	Evaluative
MIT	Strongly recommended	Evaluative
Princeton	Recommended	Evaluative
Rice	Recommended	Evaluative
Swarthmore College	Recommended	Evaluative
Trinity College	Recommended	Evaluative
Union College	Recommended	Evaluative
University of Pennsylvania	Recommended	Evaluative
Wake Forest University	Recommended	Evaluative
Wellesley	Recommended	Evaluative
Wesleyan University	Recommended	Evaluative
Yale	Recommended	Evaluative

Source: *PrepScholar* article, "The Complete List of Colleges That Require Interviews," https://blog.prepscholar.com/full-list-of-colleges-that-require-interviews

2. How to Prepare for Interviews

If you are a first-semester junior, your interviews are ahead of you, so you have adequate time to prepare for them. If you are a senior, you're now fully engaged in the application phase of your admissions campaign. But as busy as you are, you should take time, if you haven't already, to plan for your interviews.

Are you likeable? No doubt you are, but it's especially important to be perceived as likeable by interviewers—likeable *and* well informed. If you reflect these two characteristics, remain relaxed, and avoid a few common mistakes, your interviews will be successful.

3. Interview Methods and Media

Interviews are not as important as they once were because many people view them as indicative of an imbalance between the *haves* and *have-nots*. Students who have access to SAT/ACT tutors, IECs, essay counselors, and similar perquisites have an advantage over those who do not. Conducting on-campus interviews with AOs tends to increase this imbalance due to travel costs and time required away from part-time jobs, which excludes some applicants for financial reasons.

A partial solution offered by many colleges is alumni interviews. Alumni who volunteer to be regional interviewers for their alma maters are prepped on how to conduct them. Then they travel to high schools, college fairs, and other venues to interview students. Some even make house calls.

In-person conversations are the best way for an interviewer to learn about an applicant. But there are those who aren't within the range of an alumni interviewer. For these applicants, there are efficient, if less effective, media for video interviews, such as Skype, Zoom, and several other teleconferencing platforms. And, as a last resort, there's always the telephone. Get interviewed through whatever medium is available to you if you can.

4. How to Conduct Yourself

You should be as relaxed and confident as you can in your interviews. The key to being relaxed is preparation. If you are well prepared, your conversation with an interviewer will come across as natural, even if it was, in fact, rehearsed. Your high confidence level will also enable you to provide cogent ad-lib responses to questions that you didn't anticipate.

The initial step in preparation for an interview is to review everything on the college's website, including their course catalog. Become familiar with the college's mission statement. Read their recent press releases. Do a web search to find any recent media articles regarding new facilities and programs. Discreetly reflect your knowledge of the college in your conversation and questions.

Interviewers expect you to ask questions, not just answer them. To fail to ask questions may be perceived as lack of interest in their college. The first two examples below are questions that indicate that you did your research. The third example gives interviewers a chance to talk about themselves, which is something that makes people comfortable with you. The fourth question shows that you were listening when they were speaking. Your questions should always be worded to *assume the close*, which, in sales-speak, means to subtly anticipate your acceptance by the college.

"I plan to participate in the field study program in archaeology, but that may interfere with my ability to play in the orchestra. Do you know if there are other student-musicians who study abroad for their major?"

"I would like to participate in the internship program that you have for fine arts majors, but I didn't find examples of what these internships would entail. Can you give me some examples?"

"What do you know now that you wish you knew when you were an incoming freshman here?"

"Earlier, you mentioned that there are undergraduate math tutors. Can you explain to me what the qualifications are to become a tutor?"

Questions Students Should *Not* Ask

- Don't ask anything that is answered on the website.
- Don't focus on campus life to the exclusion of academics.
- Don't ask, "What are my chances for admission?"
- Don't ask so many questions that there's no time to talk about yourself.
- Don't shoot from the hip—ask each question with purpose.
- Don't ask questions that the interviewer may consider personal.

THE WAITING GAME

After the applications are submitted and interviews completed, months down the road you may face the disappointment of not having a final response from your colleges. The colleges use waitlists for the purpose of having a backup pool of acceptable candidates in case the yield is lower than expected.

In 2019, the US Department of Justice filed a suit against the National Association for College Admissions Counseling (NACAC) alleging that its rules limited competition among colleges for students. In fact, NACAC had three rules that restricted recruiting of students from other colleges. These rules were withdrawn to stop the suit. As a result, colleges can now entice transfer students from other colleges, continue to recruit students who have deposited at another college, and work toward turning non-committed students into members of their communities. This has caused the relative calm of the summer to become the Wild West. In addition to summer melt, which refers to students who have deposited to a college forfeiting that deposit to take a spot at another college who had them on the waitlist, students are now being offered incentives to violate their commitment after the May 1 deadline to come to another college. This has caused the use of waitlists to explode in the last few years with numerous colleges putting many more students on their waitlists than they can ever accept. Typically, applicants who were nearly qualified for acceptance are placed on the college waitlist to be available in case the enrollment yield from applicants who have been offered admission is lower than anticipated. The incentive for colleges to now have waitlists that can fill their class two or three times over is greater because they don't know who might actually arrive on campus in August.

The types of waitlists has also been altered. Some schools now offer a priority waitlist, which means that you are in but only if you profess to the college that if admitted you are likely to attend. Then there is the regular waitlist, which also asks if you want to stay on the waitlist or not. This is viewed as proof of your continued interest in the college.

There are also times when the waitlist is used for other reasons.

a. Some colleges wait-list the legacy students they don't plan to accept in order to not upset alumni parents.
b. Some well-qualified applicants are wait-listed so the college can gauge the student's level of interest in attending their college.
c. Some colleges use their waitlist to ensure that particular programs are filled. Try to find out if you've applied to a program that may be undersubscribed.
d. Waitlists help to ensure geographic, ethnic, and other types of diversity on campus. If there are too many of one type of candidate and not enough of another, the former is wait-listed, even though that applicant remains eligible for later admission if the diversity balance warrants it.
e. More recently, colleges are using wait lists to determine whether a student will actually attend, if admitted.

Many waitlists are ranked, meaning the college has a list of applicants who will be offered admission before you. Some of those colleges will tell you where you are ranked on their list and how far down the list they usually go in admitting waitlisted students. This can help you to determine if you want to be on their waitlist at all.

If you are wait-listed, the chances are slim that you will be admitted under most circumstances. I advise my students to only stay on the waitlist if they have a reasonable expectation of acceptance and if you really want to attend that college above the others to whom you have been accepted. You can determine this by looking at the statistics for prior year waitlist results.

Often, when an applicant has been wait-listed, the emotional attachment to that college is lessened. It makes the student feel less qualified to be part of that school's community and can affect his/her success there. If this sounds like you, politely decline the waitlist offer and enroll in a school to which you were admitted outright.

Remember that where you go to college is less important than what you do when you get there. Many extremely successful people went to colleges whose names you might not recognize. Focus on those colleges that really want you! In any case, be sure to send your deposit to one college prior to the May 1 deadline so that you are sure to have a seat. Some waitlist notifications come as late as August. Don't wait for them.

CHAPTER 12: YOUR APPLICATION—LETTERS OF RECOMMENDATION

Admission officers (AOs) view Letters of Recommendation (LORs) as one of the sources of the information they need to form a holistic picture of you. LORs present firsthand information about you that's not available elsewhere in your application. As such, AOs need LORs and the other soft factors to supplement your academic data so they can narrow the pool of applicants down to the number that they can accept. They assume that if your teachers speak glowingly and knowledgeably about you, you're more likely to succeed in their college and contribute to their programs and community.

As a key part of your application to colleges, LORs should adhere to the admissions strategy you develop, preferably in junior year or sooner. LORs with your theme embedded within them have the greatest potential to enhance your case for admission.

Your LORs will have a positive effect on admissions if you treat them as more than just items to check off your list of things to do. LORs often fail to make much of an impact on an admission officer, but that need not be so in your case. Help each of your recommenders understand and accept what you would like your LORs to communicate to colleges. The result will be LORs that mesh with your theme and the expectations of Admission Officers (AOs).

Seniors: Don't make last-minute requests and expect a great letter—or any letter at all. Give recommenders at least a month so they can produce a letter that may help your cause. It's best not to procrastinate on recommendation letter development.

Who writes your recommendations is as important as their content. Choosing carefully helps make sure that your LORs are specific, appropriate, enthusiastic, and personal. Consider the ideas below before deciding whom to ask.

1. Recommenders Should Work with You

You may have an excellent relationship with a recommender, and they may agree in junior year to write a letter for you. Don't assume that the rest of the process will take care of itself. At the end of junior year or the beginning of senior year, you should meet with each of your recommenders. Prepare documentation that includes your résumé and a memo from you that, among other things, states your theme. It should also include a reminder of how well you performed in their class or an anecdote that reflects your participation in the class. Attach a graded paper or exam. List your academic accomplishments such as your GPA, AP grades, honor rolls, college courses taken, and awards received. Name a few of the colleges that you're most interested in attending.

When you meet with a recommender, initiate a candid conversation about the personal attributes that you'd like them to highlight, other facts that you'd like them to include, and your theme. Don't ask them if they'll permit you to remind them of deadlines because they might say no. Remind them, but don't overdo it.

A good rule of thumb is to ask two teachers from eleventh or twelfth grade. One should be from English or the Humanities and the other from Math or Science. It is also helpful if the teachers have either taught you earlier in your high school career or have been involved with you as a club adviser or coach. These people can attest to your growth as a person and as a student. They can tell the college about your leadership skills and your intellectual curiosity.

2. A Recommender's Background Should Relate to Your Goals

You'll need two teacher LORs for most colleges. Your guidance counselor will also provide a recommendation. Letters from teachers in core courses are preferred—math, science, English, social science, or foreign languages. Even if it's not specifically required, it's a good idea to elicit a LOR from a teacher who has experience in your intended field of study. They'll be able to offer evidence supporting your plan to major in their specialty.

Some colleges require a LOR from a peer. Choose a peer who can personally attest not only to your character but also to your accomplishments. If you have the option of choosing a current student at the targeted college, do so. This peer can relate your personality and interests in a way that ties them to that college. S/he can provide relevance by expressing why you'd be a good fit for the institution. Some colleges ask you to submit a LOR from an outside recommender, such as a summer course college professor, coach, pastor, leader of a volunteer organization, or your manager at a job. Handle those requests the same way you would a teacher.

3. Recommenders Should Know You Well

Much of what makes asking for LORs so challenging is that you don't know exactly what the person who agrees to write the LOR will actually write. For best results, get to know your recommenders early in junior year to build a rapport with them. Junior-year teachers, not senior-year teachers, are considered by AOs to be the ones who know you best because they've taught you for a full academic year. By starting in junior year, you'll be able to influence teachers to write LORs that embed your theme so that they'll mesh with your essays, personal statements, and interviews.

It's also a good idea to try to set up a 10-minute meeting with your guidance counselor once or twice a year starting in sophomore year. Use this opportunity to politely keep them up to date on your plans and progress and ask for their advice. Also, guidance counselors need not inform you when they've sent a recommendation to a college, so check with them prior to deadlines.

Many colleges will not accept more than their required number of LORs. For those that will accept and evaluate supplemental LORs, consider asking an English teacher (if you haven't already). Admission officers know that competent writing is a key to success in all majors.

CHAPTER 13: SPECIAL POPULATIONS

This chapter is a guide for those applicants who are, in some important way, different from the general population of college applicants. Under certain circumstances, these characteristics can be used to enhance your attractiveness as an applicant. In all cases, your admissions campaign should differ from the standard approach recommended in this book in order to adjust for *your* circumstances and characteristics.

The types of students considered to be special populations in this book are:

1. First-generation students
2. LGBTQ+ students
3. Students with disabilities,
4. Undocumented immigrant students
5. Students from historically underrepresented minorities
6. Asian Americans
7. International students
8. Hispanic/LatinX students

Chapter 2: Affording College includes descriptions of the types of scholarships, grants, work-study, and loan programs that are available to students applying to or attending college. Students in special populations and their parents should investigate these sources of funding for their potential to assist in paying for college. In addition to programs that are available to all applicants, there are many financial assistance opportunities that are only available to members of one or more of the special populations.

1. First-Generation Students

There are several definitions of a first-generation student:

- Neither parent has obtained a bachelor's or graduate degree.
- Neither parent has obtained an associate degree.
- Neither parent has obtained a college-issued certificate.
- Neither a parent nor a sibling has ever enrolled in college.

The Free Application for Federal Student Aid (FAFSA) uses the least restrictive of these definitions, which is the first one, as the definition of a first-generation student. Private scholarships programs may use any of the other definitions. You should ascertain if you're eligible under the program rules of each financial aid program to which you apply.

There are many scholarship programs that target first-generation students. The scholarship-finding services in Chapter 2: Affording College will provide valuable assistance in finding other programs for which you're eligible. A partial list is provided below.

- American Indian College Fund
- Coca-Cola First Generation Grants
- Buick Achievers Scholarship
- Center for Student Opportunity "I'm First!" Scholarship
- Chicago Public Schools—Choose Your Future Scholarship Fund
- Cynthia E. Morgan Memorial Scholarship Fund
- Florida First Generation Matching Grant

- Institute for Study Abroad—First Generation College Student Program
- Norman and Pat Hayes Scholarship
- Patty & Melvin Alperin First Generation Scholarship
- Smith Scholarship Foundation
- Talent Incentive Program Grants
- TMCF/Walmart First-Generation Scholarship Program
- TELACU Education Foundation College Success Program
- TELACU Education Foundation Graduate School Support
- VAMOS Scholarships

Many colleges have their own institutional scholarships for first-generation college students. Examples include the following:

- Benjamin and Patricia Allen Scholarship for first generation college students at Iowa State University
- First Generation Grant at the University of Colorado at Boulder
- Frederik Meijer First Generation Honors Scholarship at Grand Valley State University
- Ingrid Saunders Jones Endowed Scholarship Fund at Michigan State University
- Fannie & Sam Constantino First Generation Scholarship at St. John Fisher College
- The Student Support Services Scholars Academy and the George A. Miller Scholars Program at UC Berkeley
- Regents' Scholarship at Texas A&M University

First-generation college students have a graduation rate of only 34 percent compared to 55 percent for the general undergraduate population. This low graduation rate is due mainly to the lack of sufficient funding coupled with insufficient academic support, like mentoring and tutoring programs. A range of programs intended to provide funding and academic support exist to help you manage the many variables that confront you as a freshman first-generation student. It's well worth your effort to start pursuing them in your junior year. Such programs can be located via a web search engine, but I've listed a few below.

a. **College Greenlight:** Creating a free profile on College Greenlight, which was developed for both first-generation and low-income students, gives you access to a searchable database of more than $11 billion worth of scholarships for which you may be eligible.
b. **Strive for College:** If you're struggling to get started with a scholarship search, Strive for College can be a good resource. Using the UStrive platform, you can meet with a mentor online who can answer your questions about scholarships. Your mentor will help you find the best scholarships for you. Strive for College reports that 89 percent of its student clients attend college without incurring any student loan debt. Teaching you how to apply for financial aid is also a big part of the nonprofit's free online curriculum.
c. **FirstGEN Fellows:** Designed for first-generation students who want to pursue a career in social justice, FirstGEN Fellows awards a one-time stipend of $1,500 per student. In addition to the award, six of the Fellows take part in a ten-week summer program of internships in the federal government in Washington, D.C.
d. **Student Success Agency:** First-generation students can benefit from having someone help them determine how to pay for college. That's the purpose of the Student Success Agency. The agency says that 90 percent of its student clients receive scholarships from over 30 US colleges. In addition to finding scholarships, Student Success agents help students to apply to colleges. The agency estimates that the average student/agent pair interacts about 45 times per month. Unlike other support organizations for first-generation students, the agency charges a fee. To be paired with an agent, your cost is $65 per month.

2. LGBTQ+ Students

The college admissions process can induce high anxiety in any young person. If you're in the LGBTQ+ community, you may experience an even higher level of anxiety. You're not sure until you get there what degree of LGBTQ+ friendliness awaits you. For this reason, you should research the schools that initially make your

College List to verify that they'll welcome you and other LGBTQ+ students. If you get bad vibes, drop them.

Until the last two decades or so, applying to colleges was harrowing for LGBTQ+ students. They had to cope with the issue of whether or not to identify their sexual orientation in, say, essays or interviews. Usually the answer was no, and the reason was obvious. Why take an unnecessary risk if your objective is to secure admission in a competitive field of applicants? Applicants never knew the real reason why admission officers might put their application aside.

Sexual orientation is now a non-issue in admissions. LGBTQ+ applicants can feel free to self-identify without fear of repercussions. The Supreme Court in 2020 affirmed that LGBTQ+ individuals are entitled to the full protection of Title VII of the Civil Rights Act of 1964, which prohibits discrimination on account of sex.

Many colleges now invite students to disclose, as an option, their sexual orientation, gender identity, and preferred pronouns in their application supplements. Certain schools such as the University of Pennsylvania have gone even further and announced that they are inclined to use information about sexual orientation to recruit LGBTQ+ students in pursuit of their mission to optimize the diversity of their student population.

Not everyone agrees with the openness of the UPenn approach. The Common App Board has declined to include a question about sexual orientation on the Common App itself. Their reasoning is that high school students are too young to respond with certainty to a question about sexual orientation—a response that will remain on the record. Even applicants who are certain of their orientation often prefer to keep it confidential. Supporting this viewpoint is Adam Chandler who, as a Yale undergraduate, knew he was gay but chose not to come out.

"So as more and more colleges ask a question that is premature and impolite, what makes their inquiry truly nefarious is the quandary it represents for closeted applicants: Should they disclose their most closely held secret to increase their odds of admission?"

—Adam Chandler

Table 13A, below, is a review of colleges considered to be LGBTQ+ inclusive that also have a reputation for high academic quality.

Table 13A: Colleges Most Welcoming to LGBTQ+ Students

#1 Bryn Mawr College	#11 Nazareth College
#2 Mount Holyoke College	#12 Scripps College
#3 Franklin W. Olin College of Engineering	#13 Pitzer College
#4 Brown University	#14 Mills College
#5 Agnes Scott College	#15 Columbia University
#6 College of the Atlantic	#16 Macalester College
#7 Reed College	#17 Emerson College
#8 Wellesley College	#18 William & Mary
#9 Rice University	#19 Wesleyan University
#10 The University of North Carolina at Asheville	#20 State University of New York - Purchase College

Source: https://www.princetonreview.com/college-rankings?rankings=lgbtq-friendly 4/11/2021

- If you're evaluating the LBGTQ+ friendliness of a college on your own, here are some factors that may indicate that you'll be comfortable attending the school:
- There are clearly written nondiscrimination policies in place.
- There is a vibrant LGBTQ+ student social life.
- Options exist for LGBTQ+ courses in the curriculum of different majors.
- The college has gender-inclusive residences and restrooms.
- Specific health care options for LGBTQ+ students exist.
- Suitable campus safety training and procedures are in place.

3. Students with Disabilities

College life can be challenging for freshmen, especially for the disabled. Disabled students need to find appropriate programs for their assistance and support while the pace of their education greatly accelerates.

Certain colleges go above and beyond the ordinary to make the transition to college life easier for those with disabilities. They raise the awareness of students and faculty to get them involved in making daily life more convenient for those new students who are disabled. Finding these colleges among the 4,000 or so in the United States should be an objective of the admissions campaigns of disabled students.

The American with Disabilities Act of 1990 (ADA) was a landmark law for those suffering from discrimination at colleges due to the institutions' lack of preparedness to accommodate the disabled. As a result of the law, colleges were required to build facilities and programs that were accessible by disabled students on an equal basis with the nondisabled.

Today, most campuses feature power-accessible doors, wheelchair ramps, elevators, curb cuts, and a range of other features that make the daily life of physically disabled students easier. Nevertheless, a recent survey of colleges conducted by the University of Connecticut found that, although 86 percent of colleges enroll students with disabilities, only 24 percent of them say they offer special assistance "to a major extent."

The two major types of disabilities, physical and learning, are different. They're sufficiently dissimilar enough to require distinctly different approaches to assistance and support. Certain colleges excel in accommodating the disabled, some with physically disabled individuals and others with the learning disabled.

a. **Physical Disabilities** There are well over one million physically disabled undergraduates in the United States, based on data from the last national census. This represents 6 percent of all undergraduates. Although they must be ADA-compliant, many colleges don't fully meet the needs of the physically disabled. This is particularly true for those students with disabilities so serious that they have a comprehensive impact on daily life.

The colleges listed below, according to several sources, have consistently prioritized the social, academic, and accessibility needs of students with physical disabilities. The majority of these campuses have centers for the disabled that are professionally staffed. They provide needed services and assistive technology. They also conduct programs to foster the academic success of the disabled.

Table 13B: Best Colleges for Students with Physical Disabilities

1. BALL STATE UNIVERSITY	6. UNIVERSITY OF FLORIDA
2. UNIVERSITY OF ILLINOIS AT URBANA–CHAMPAIGN	7. RAMAPO COLLEGE OF NEW JERSEY
3. WRIGHT STATE UNIVERSITY	8. SOUTHERN ILLINOIS UNIVERSITY CARBONDALE
4. EDINBORO UNIVERSITY	9. UNIVERSITY OF MISSOURI
5. UNIVERSITY OF CALIFORNIA–BERKELEY	10. NORTHERN KENTUCKY UNIVERSITY

Source: https://www.collegemagazine.com/top-10-campuses-for-students-with-physical-disabilities/ 4/11/2021

b. **Learning Disabilities** A learning disability is a clinical diagnosis for which the individual must meet certain criteria as determined by a psychologist, speech pathologist, pediatrician, psychiatrist, or a similarly qualified professional. Sometimes referred to as learning disorders, the most common of them are dyslexia, which is difficulty in reading, dyscalculia, which is difficulty with arithmetic, and dysgraphia, which is difficulty in handwriting. Autism may be considered a learning disability depending upon where an individual is on the spectrum.

The colleges listed below, according to several sources, have consistently prioritized the needs of students with learning disabilities.

Table 13C: Best Colleges for Students with Learning Disabilities

1. Beacon College	11. DePaul University
2. Landmark College	12. Ursuline College
3. Hofstra University	13. University of California–Irvine
4. Adelphi University	14. Ashland University
5. University of North Carolina–Chapel Hill	15. Mitchell College
6. Marshall University	16. American University
7. The University of Arizona	17. University of Connecticut
8. University of the Ozarks	18. Northeastern University
9. West Virginia Wesleyan College	19. University of Denver
10. Daemen College	20. Roosevelt University

Source: https://www.petersons.com/blog/20-great-colleges-for-students-with-learning-disabilities/ 4/11/2021

c. **Finding the Right College** Rather than relying on a list, you may prefer to decide for yourself which colleges are best for you. The guidelines below can help you in this effort.

- **Prepare Early:** As a disabled student, you should start checking out the capabilities of colleges regarding the disabled early in high school. For example, you can research your colleges of interest to see if they offer support groups, clubs, adaptive sports, and/or a center for the disabled.
- **Visit Colleges:** Accommodations for disabled students may not always be what they are purported to be on a college's website. Buildings erected before the passing of the ADA may be "grandfathered" and exempt from the law. Some older institutions, particularly in the Northeast, remain difficult to navigate despite the best efforts of the colleges. Other colleges may tout their disability-friendliness but prove otherwise during your visit. Nevertheless, campus visits are highly recommended to find out what's real and what's not. The recent upgrading of virtual college tours brought about by the pandemic will benefit you as a way to become familiar with campuses you can't visit. Many colleges offer customized virtual tours that involve a student with a smartphone who tours the campus and shows you whatever you request to see.
- **High School Isn't College:** Don't assume that colleges will all accommodate disabilities in the same way that your high school did. The K–12 system is required to follow the Individuals with Disabilities Education Act (IDEA) but colleges follow the Americans with Disabilities Act (ADA) Guidelines. Most high schools follow state and federal regulations to the letter. Many colleges are private institutions and, as such, they have more leeway in how they comply with regulations. You shouldn't use your high school as the standard for all colleges. Some won't make the grade.
- **Documentation:** You should contact the Office of Disabled Services at a college you might attend to ask that they provide documentation for any program that affects your disability. Normally, your testing documentation must be less than three

years old. You will want to receive all of the services that they offer if you go there.

- **Be Your Own Advocate:** Most disabled students prefer not to threaten action against a professor or administrative manager who isn't complying with the college's policies regarding disabled students. It's difficult to convince such a person that what they're doing is wrong. Also, if they are faculty, they determine your grade. But being assertive is sometimes the best approach to a difficult situation. Gently present your case to the person in private without threatening action. If the result disappoints you, elevate your complaint to an appropriate forum for resolution.

d. **Scholarships for Disabled Students** Physical disabilities no longer present barriers to admission. Although many of the factors that once discouraged physically disabled students from pursuing a college education have been mitigated or eliminated, the high cost of college is still a barrier to many. Fortunately, there are scholarships that are designated specifically for students with disabilities.

Although colleges aren't required to provide financial assistance to disabled students, most do. In addition, there are many scholarships for students with disabilities from external, noninstitutional sources. These can be difficult to find even if you're using the popular online scholarship locators (see Chapter 2: Affording College). However, there is a listing of scholarships available, organized by the nature of the disability, at www.scholarships.com. You should review this website and apply for scholarships for which you're qualified.

Numerous scholarships are also offered only to students with learning disabilities. This is particularly important since many colleges charge fees for services to these students above the cost of tuition. These scholarships can alleviate the financial strain associated with college. For a directory, please refer to http://www.finaid.org.

4. Undocumented Immigrant Students

There are about 700,000 people who were born in other countries and immigrated as children to this country with their parents while undocumented. Deferred Action for Childhood Arrivals (DACA) is a US immigration policy that, since 2012, allows these individuals—known as Dreamers—to receive renewable two-year deferments from deportation. During this deferment, they are eligible for work permits and may enroll in college. To qualify as a Dreamer, a person must have entered the United States before they were 16 years old and have been less than 31 years old by mid 2012.

In June of 2020, the Supreme Court ruled that a federal executive order issued in 2017 to rescind the DACA policy was in violation of US Administrative Law. Even if the 2017 executive order is corrected and reissued, proponents of DACA have about a year to generate additional support for its extension as a policy or enactment into law. Such a law would provide for a path to citizenship for Dreamers instead of deportation. Early in 2021, further changes were made to make the path to citizenship easier for Dreamers to follow.

There are other types of undocumented immigrants seeking higher education in the United States who don't fit the definition of Dreamers:

- Students who immigrated with parents since 2012 and are undocumented.
- Students who immigrated alone to live with unofficial guardians
- Students who immigrated unaccompanied by adults to reunite with parents

The situation for these undocumented students varies by state. *Plyler v. Doe* (1982) grants undocumented students the right to a K–12 education but not a college education. However, there is no federal law that prohibits undocumented students from attending a public college. State legislation either supports or restricts access to colleges to undocumented students. Only two states, South Carolina and Alabama, ban enrollment to undocumented students without exception. Other states have tuition equity laws that prohibit discrimination against undocumented students. The policies of the other states fall in between these two extremes. Private colleges are free to admit undocumented students at their discretion.

If you are a Dreamer or fit into one of the other groups listed above, there are scholarship and services programs to assist you in applying and paying for college. Many of these can be found through the free online scholarship finders noted in Chapter 2: Affording College. Let these search engines filter the universe of scholarships down to those for undocumented immigrants.

The National Association of College Admissions Counseling (NACAC) offers a guide titled *Best Practices for Supporting Undocumented Students*. The publication is free to download from http://www.nacacnet.org.

5. Students from Historically Underrepresented Minorities (URMs)

The definition of a URM student is one whose racial or ethnic background consists of any of the following:

- African American/Black
- Asian: Only Filipino or Vietnamese (including Hmong)
- Hispanic/Latinx
- Native American/Alaskan Native
- Native Hawaiian/Pacific Islander

a. Diversity In the past, members of these groups would have been at a disadvantage in college admissions. However, since the enactment of the *Civil Rights Act of 1964*, which prohibited racial and ethnic discrimination, they are no longer disadvantaged in admissions by discrimination.

The Supreme Court, in a series of decisions, ruled that Affirmative Action was inherently discriminatory and therefore couldn't be used by public or private educational institutions that accept federal funds, which is essentially all of them. But the Supreme Court has also consistently maintained that colleges may seek diversity in their student population as a worthy goal because it helps to prepare students for life in a diverse society.

Many colleges have, as part of their mission, the achievement of a diverse student body. This is especially true at top-tier institutions. The role of diversity in admissions is usually positive for minority students.

b. **Scholarships and Counseling for URM Students** URM students are far scarcer at US colleges than a general population *pro rata* representation would dictate. There are many reasons for their lower enrollment and graduation rates, but the most prominent are financial hardship and the lack of educational counseling.

   To make college education more accessible to URM students, hundreds of public and private organizations offer scholarships and financial aid programs for them. If you're a URM student, you should thoroughly review the opportunities available to you. Several websites maintain free scholarship listings that are set aside for URM students. NACAC and the Independent Educational Consultants Association (IECA), another widely supported professional association, maintain lists of professional college admissions counselors who provide *pro bono* services to URM students.

6. Asian American Students

Asian American students who aren't of Filipino or Vietnamese descent aren't considered to be URMs. Some of these students have complained that, as a minority, they are the victims of discrimination by colleges, especially top-tier institutions, that use diversity as a shield to avoid compliance with laws such as the Civil Rights Act.

Highlighting this controversy is a court case heard last year in a US District Court in Boston: *Students for Fair Admission, Inc. v. President and Fellows of Harvard College. Students* is a group of Asian American students who were rejected as applicants to Harvard. They claimed that Harvard intentionally discriminated against Asian American applicants and engaged in unfair racial balancing. The court ultimately ruled in favor of Harvard, which has been construed as reaffirming the validity of race-conscious admissions as a means of assembling a diverse freshmen class. The decision has been appealed, and it is expected that the US Supreme Court will ultimately decide the case. (See the sidebar below for more details).

Regardless of the outcome, this case demonstrates that the use of race as a factor in admissions remains controversial. Minority students who seek to use this characteristic of their background as leverage in admissions are still free to do so, but the window for using race or ethnicity may be closing.

In its defense, Harvard claimed it takes steps to assemble a socioeconomically, geographically, racially, and ethnically diverse freshman class. Low-income applicants, minorities, and rural applicants get a boost in admissions due to what's referred to as their personal rating. Harvard said race can be a plus for Asian American applicants but never a negative factor in admissions. The institution maintained that race is only one factor among many factored into admissions decisions.

The most disputed issue in Harvard's testimony is the *personal rating*. The plaintiff alleged that being Asian American is detrimental even though race itself is *never* explicitly considered as a discrete factor. The plaintiff claimed that discrimination is statistically irrefutable, and that Harvard has an implicit quota of Asian American students because they want to avoid a situation in which the majority of students are Asian American. This is what happened at top-tier race-blind institutions such as UC–Berkeley. As a motive, the plaintiff asserted that a disproportionally high percentage of Asian American students would hurt Harvard's ability to favor legacy applicants. This would constrain the growth of the college's endowment fund. It also might discourage many well-qualified students from applying to Harvard.

Harvard is accused of knowingly discriminating against Asian Americans via the personal rating because it assesses character and personality. It rewards traits such as "courage," "likeability," and "leadership," as gleaned from applications, interviews, essays, and letters of recommendation. Due to the dominant methods of upbringing associated with different racial groups, the plaintiff alleged, Asian Americans are rated as so similar in type that it interferes with their ability to serve Harvard's mission of student diversity. For example, most Asian Americans are rated as more studious, less demonstrative, introverted, and reluctant to assume leadership than their non-Asian peers. As summed up in the Los Angeles Times, "Harvard University intentionally uses a vague 'personal rating' to reject Asian American applicants in favor of students from other racial backgrounds."

7. International Students

Europeans have long admired American institutions of higher learning. Through the years, many affluent parents from these countries have enrolled their children in US colleges, especially top-tier universities. In recent decades, globalization and rapid modernization have enabled many students from affluent families in Asia, especially India and China, to be able to afford American colleges. As a result, the number of international students enrolled at American colleges and universities has risen sharply in the last decade.

Since demand for admission is so high among international students, competition is intense. As an international student, you must contend with an arduous process to apply to American colleges. You must also deal with a complex visa system.

If you aspire to attend college in the United States, there are several steps that you'll need to take in order to be successful. Since it can be complicated, start the process as early as you can. Here's a breakdown of the three most important aspects of your effort: admission, funding, and visas.

a. **Admission** Colleges in the United States require applicants from non-English speaking countries to take an English as a Second Language (ESL) test. Two common examples are the Test of English as a Foreign Language (TOEFL) and the International English Language Testing System (IELTS). You'll also need to take the SAT or the ACT for undergraduate admission. Both are offered periodically in many international cities. You should take your exams about 18 months before you plan to begin college.

The application submission deadline for the early decision (ED) round of admissions can be as early as November 1. You may wish to apply to your first-choice college via the ED cycle because the admission rate may be higher than in the regular decision (RD) process. If you're accepted in the ED round, you are legally bound to attend that institution, so you should only apply via ED to an institution that you are sure you want to attend above all others. The deadline for submission of applications for RD varies between January 1 and as late as March. You'll be informed of the college's decision in the last week of March or early April.

The Common Application (Common App) is a standard form that many US colleges accept in order to save the time and effort of applicants and to simplify their own processing. It's initially available online every August 1 for the academic year that begins in the fall of the following year. The Common App organization recognizes that the admissions process will take you a year or more.

A typical application that you submit to an American college via the Common App, which includes a personal statement and an essay that responds to one of the Common App's several essay prompts. Usually, two letters of recommendation that must be sent directly to the college from faculty members and one from your guidance counselor. Your high school must send a transcript of your academic record directly to colleges. Your school counselor can send the recommendations and transcript either directly from the Common App or through its connection to Naviance. The student is responsible to send his or her SAT/ACT scores directly to colleges. As an international student, you'll also arrange to have your ESL test score sent directly to colleges. Certain colleges have supplemental requirements that most often consist of essays that respond to their own set of prompts.

b. **Funding** American universities offer two types of funding: need-based and merit-based. Need-based funding is generally reserved for American students. Scholarships, which reward academic excellence or extracurricular talent, are extremely competitive for international students. It's more common for an international student to secure institutional funding after their first year of study at a college. Any scholarships awarded will only partially cover the cost of tuition and may obligate the student to work for the college part-time under the funding agreement.

One factor that favors international students in admissions is that, because funding is rarely available to them, they usually pay the full cost of tuition, whereas most American students have had their tuition discounted of one reason or another. This makes international students more attractive to US colleges than Americans from a revenue perspective.

American students submit the FAFSA, which provides a financial profile of the family in order to determine the extent of the student's financial need. This form asks questions that cannot be answered by an international student and his or her family, especially on tax-related matters. In its place, an international family may submit a financial statement that provides information in several categories as requested by a college.

Some scholarships are designated for applicants with specific characteristics, such as country of origin, ethnicity, faith, gender, academic interests, and talents. The Education USA financial aid search tool can help you find suitable funding opportunities to which you may apply.

c. **Visas** There are three types of visas for international students in the United States: F1 for academic studies; J1 for practical training not available in your home country; and M1 for vocational studies.

If you are applying for an academic degree, you'll need an F1 visa—the most common one used by international students. With certain exceptions, you'll be obligated to return to your home country within 60 days of completing your degree. You'll have to pay a visa application fee and must have already been accepted at a US college when you apply for the visa. Your visa is only valid to study at that specific college; while it is possible to transfer to another college, there are more forms to fill out and steps to take. You'll need to have a visa interview with a representative of the US government at which you'll be required to prove that you have sufficient funds to support your stay. You'll also need to prove strong ties to your home country through family connections, assets, bank accounts, or other factors. The visa allows you to work part time in the United States during your studies.

If you want to stay in the United States for up to 12 months after your studies, the Optional Practical Training (OPT) program allows international students on F1 visas to do so if they obtain employment in their field of study. Graduates in the fields of science, technology, engineering, or mathematics can extend their OPT by an additional 17 months, meaning that they may stay in the United States for more than two years to work in their field. You must apply for OPT before completing your degree program.

The J1 visa applies to specialist programs that provide training that you cannot otherwise obtain in your home country. Examples include a business trainee program, an internship with a large corporation, or a physician's assistant program. Some of these programs involve college study, but many involve practical training. For the most part, you won't be able to apply for a J1 visa to study in the United States unless there's an existing agreement with the intended employer and your government.

The M1 visa is for vocational studies. Students cannot work at a full-time job on an M1 visa, although they can take part-time work if it's relevant to their studies. The

M1 visa is only available to students at a qualified trade or technical school, so find out beforehand if the school that you're applying to is qualified.

d. **If You're Rejected** If you're an international student who has been rejected by the American colleges to which you've applied, you are free to keep on trying. You may wish to change your approach. The United States has over 4,000 colleges and universities. This means that you can apply to any number of additional colleges—a task made simpler by the Common App. Application fees for American colleges should not impede this approach because they average only $41. The most important thing that you can do is to find those colleges that fit your needs and preferences best.

   Here are a few options for you as an international student who hasn't yet gained admission to a US college:

   - Wait one full academic year and try again next year. Retake any exams on which your scores may have been inadequate. Take college courses at home without enrolling so that you can prove your ability to perform college-level work.
   - Apply immediately to several American colleges with rolling admissions. Many US colleges offer rolling admissions and accept applications through July and early August. Rolling admissions means students can apply at any time after a college begins accepting applications in the fall. The college will evaluate all applications as they're received. Applications are viewed especially favorably if the admissions office hasn't yet reached its target number of enrolled applicants.
   - Enroll at an American two-year community college and transfer to a four-year college after graduation. Community colleges have application deadlines that are usually one month before classes start. Many community colleges offer a simplified application process. If you cannot begin your studies in the fall, a community college will let you begin in the spring semester so that you don't have to wait

an entire academic year. You can expect an admissions decision from a community college within two weeks. Your ability to transfer to a four-year college after graduation is not guaranteed under an F1 visa, but you can resolve this matter if you start early. Community college guidance counselors are familiar with this issue and will be able to assist you.

CHAPTER 14: RESOURCES FOR YOUR RESERACH

Students need accurate information to guide them in finding the colleges that fit them best, so I'm often asked which resources are most helpful for this purpose. There are several types of excellent resources available to you in conducting your research.

1. Subjective Guides

Subjective guides are useful in assessing how comfortable you are likely to feel at a particular college. A good example is the *Fiske Guide*, which provides essay-like two- or three-page summaries of each school. It includes information about the academic programs, popular majors, intellectual climate, physical campus, accessibility of professors, athletics, social environment, and the geographic area in which the school is located. The staff of the *Yale Daily News* also publishes the *Insider's Guide to Colleges*, which is a similar compilation of insider views of colleges. I strongly recommend that your research include subjective guides because they provide a sense of what a college is really like.

2. Objective Guides

In addition to subjective considerations, you'll also want a statistical profile of colleges. You need to be aware of what incoming freshmen are like by various academic measures. The *Complete Book of Colleges* from the *Princeton Review* has a great deal of helpful information for applicants that you should review in order to decide which colleges are right for you. The *Profile of American Colleges* from *Barron's* has substantial information about the competitiveness of admissions at colleges.

3. Magazine Rankings

Among the resources that don't fit neatly into the two categories above are the college rankings issues of magazines. The most widely referenced of these is the annual edition of the *U.S. News & World Report of Best Colleges,* with rankings of colleges in several different categories. Rankings based on the same common database but ordered according to different proprietary algorithms also are published annually by *Barron's, Forbes, Kiplinger's, Money, Princeton Review, Washington Monthly,* and others.

I advise you not to take magazine rankings too literally. They're far from definitive; at best, they can give you an indication of a college's relative overall merits. Still, they can be a jumping-off point to consider a college's reputation in the context of its peer institutions as well as its degree of selectivity, which is a key factor in rankings.

Don't use any magazine's rankings as the sole basis for your choice of colleges. The publishers may be well intentioned, but their rankings are based only on quantitative data. Your college choices should be based primarily on the personal preferences that you have established for yourself (see Chapter 5: Your Personal Preferences).

4. The College Cooperative Database

The magazine publishers referred to above all base their rankings on the same source of information—a shared database called the Common Data Set (CDS). CDS is a collaboration between publishers and colleges to maintain the quality and consistency of reported information. CDS is available for your personal research. To find the CDS data for a college, enter "Common Data Set *Name of College*" into a web search engine.

5. The Federal Government

The *College Scorecard* is a web-based resource maintained by the US Department of Education for your use in comparing the cost and value of colleges. It provides information in the following categories: programs and degrees, location, size, mission, and type of college.

6. College Websites

Be sure to thoroughly review the websites of colleges to which you might apply. This primary resource, while presented through the college administration's bias, offers a wealth of information about the academics and social opportunities at a college. You'll learn about admissions requirements, core curricula, courses in your planned major, athletic facilities, dining plans, residential options, campus amenities, and many more characteristics of the college. But keep in mind that a college's website isn't objective. It is a marketing tool. As such, its purpose is not only to disseminate relevant information about the college but to encourage you to apply. A discouraging word will never be found on any college's website.

7. Campus Visits

Campus visits aren't a passive source of information like the resources above, but they are the best basis for the comparison of colleges (see Chapter 6: Campus Visits). It is not easy to get a realistic sense of a campus unless it's based on firsthand information. Walk around, visit the dining areas, see the classrooms, and talk to lots of people. Go on an official tour, find things out on your own, or both. Visit colleges close to home before visiting those more distant. This will give you a feel for the type of campus that satisfies your preferences before you undertake the time and expense of distant visits.

In recent years, great strides have been made in the improvement of virtual tours. Many colleges use state-of-the-art virtual technology to make their tours as helpful to prospective applicants as possible. An innovative type of tour involves a current student with a smartphone virtually escorting you on your smartphone to all the usual tour stops plus those that you request to see. It's not the same as being there, but it helps you to assess a campus that you can't visit in person.

Glossary

Our friends at the College Planning Center, who produce the TrackIt Curriculum which I have used with all my students for many years, generated this comprehensive list of admissions-related terms.

Academic Index (AI): College administrators devise an algorithm that incorporates what they think are the proper weights to assign to factors in the academic records of applicants. The college will then compute a score known as an Academic Index for all applicants. The college determines what point on this scale is high enough for an applicant to be eligible for admission.

Academic Record: This consists of a high school student's GPA, SAT or ACT scores, and, in some cases, class rank. The GPA is often adjusted to take into account AP, IB, and Honors courses and exams in which a high grade was received.

Accreditation: The recognition by an outside agency that a school maintains high standards, which enables students to qualify for admission to other accredited institutions

Admission Officer (AO): The college admission representative who reviews your application

Admission Requirements: A set of rules established by each college for a student to be accepted

Advanced Placement (AP): A system by which college freshmen may bypass entry-level courses by proving that they have already taken the equivalent in high school; credit may be awarded if a student earns a certain grade on an AP exam taken in high school.

AP Scholar: Awards recognizing high school students that demonstrate college-level achievement through the AP courses and exams

Advanced Standing: Admission status when a student has completed more than 12 college credits

Aid Package: A combination of aid (scholarships, grants, loans, and work study) determined by the college financial aid office

American College Test (ACT): A four-year college admission test covering English, math, reading, and science

Associate of Arts (AA) Degree: A two-year degree with a humanities emphasis that is usually earned at a community college

Associate of Science (AS) Degree: A two-year degree with a science emphasis that is usually earned at a community college

Audit: To attend a class for the purpose of reviewing the information; no grades or credits are given.

Bachelor's Degree: The degree awarded for completing a college program of at least four years of academic work; usually this degree is either a bachelor of arts (BA) or a bachelor of science (BS).

College Board: A nonprofit organization that provides tests and many other educational services for students, schools, and colleges

College Catalog: A publication by a college describing services and courses offered, as well as requirements for admission and degrees; the college counselor at your high school may have a selection of college catalogs that includes college addresses.

Coalition for Access, Affordability, and Success: A group of public and private colleges and universities collaborating to improve the college application process; developed an online platform to streamline the process

College Scholarship Service (CSS) Profile: A financial aid form used by many private colleges to award private, nonfederal funds

Common Core Curriculum: A national initiative that specifies what high school students should know at each grade level and describes the skills that they must acquire in order to achieve college or career readiness

Credit(also called semester hours, unit hours, quarter hours, or unit): It's a way of referring to credits earned in a course. If a class meets three hours per week, it is usually a three-credit course. A full-time college student is usually defined as one who attends three to four classes and earns at least 12 credits per semester or quarter.

Cumulative Record: The complete record of all courses and grades earned; a student transcript is a copy of his/her cumulative record.

Degree: A diploma given as official recognition for satisfactory completion of a course of study; a four-year degree is usually a BA (bachelor of arts) or BS (bachelor of science). A fifth- or sixth-year degree is often a MA (master of arts) or MS (master of science.) A doctoral degree (PhD) requires five or more years beyond the BA/BS.

Early Action (EA): Highly qualified candidates who apply early may receive offers of college admission by mid-December. An Early Action plan does not allow an institution to request an applicant make a prior commitment to matriculate, indicate college preferences, or make any response to an offer of admission until the traditional candidates reply date (usually in May).

Early Decision (ED): Some colleges offer to notify applicants of acceptance or rejection during the first semester of their senior year. There are two types of early decision plans: the single-choice plan—in which students cannot apply to another college until they have been notified by the early decision college—and the first-choice plan, in which students may apply to other colleges but name the early decision college as their first choice and agree to enroll at that college and withdraw all other applications if accepted. For further information, contact the college admission office.

Economically Disadvantaged: Any individual or family whose annual earnings meet the US Department of Labor definition of low income

Elective: A course needed for graduation credit, but one that does not meet a specific course requirement

Fee Waiver: A form available to students whose eligibility is primarily determined by membership in a family with annual income falling within guidelines based on number of dependents and family income; the fee waiver is submitted instead of money when applying for college testing or admission.

Financial Aid: Scholarships, loans, grants, and/or a part-time job given to a student with financial need; the "financial aid package" of funds is determined by family financial need and the availability of college or government funds.

Financial Need: The difference between your SAI and the school's COA, also known as financial aid eligibility

Free Application for Federal Student Aid (FAFSA): The federal application form required to apply for financial aid, including grants, loans, and work-study programs.

Full-Time Student: Generally, a college student who takes a minimum of either 12 units per quarter or semester; this minimum number of units is usually required to maintain financial eligibility.

General Educational Development Examination (GED): A series of tests that adults or students aged 18 (17 1/2) or older take to qualify for a high school equivalency certificate or diploma; some colleges will accept satisfactory GED test results in place of a high school diploma. Students may not take the GED until they are at least 17. A letter of permission from the high school is required.

General Education Requirements: A specific group of courses from different academic areas required for any degree at some colleges; the general education requirements are described in each college catalog; also called Breadth Requirements.

Grade Point Average (GPA): The average number of grade points earned divided by the number of credits attempted

Grants: Financial aid that does not need to be repaid; usually awarded based on need, but can be awarded for academic achievement, special skill, talent, heritage or other criteria

Impacted Program or Major: An overcrowded program or major in which there are many more applications than available spaces; supplementary admissions criteria often must be met for consideration.

International Baccalaureate (IB): A course of study that allows high school students to satisfy admission requirements of universities in more than 70 countries; students can earn university credit for scores of 5 or higher on 1B higher-level examinations.

Liberal Arts College: A college in which the emphasis is on a program of philosophy, literature, history, languages, and basic science

Lower Division: The courses usually taken during the first two years of a four-year college program; the classes are usually introductory or general education requirements.

Major: A student's main field of study in college

Master's Degree: The degree given for completing a one- to two-year course of study beyond a bachelor's degree. Some master's degrees are master of arts (MA), master of science (MS), master of business administration (MBA), and master of fine arts (MFA).

Minor: A subject-area emphasis earned by completing approximately 18 credits in an area outside a student's major

Part-Time Student: A college student who takes less than a full-time (12 units) schedule of classes and is ineligible for many financial aid programs

Pell Grant: Financial aid from the federal government available to students with significant financial need, to be used at many types of colleges and vocational schools

Preliminary Scholastic Aptitude Test/National Merit Scholarship Qualifying Test (PSAT/NMSQT): A shortened version of the SAT offered in October to high school juniors and below; the scores are helpful in college admission planning and/or qualifying for National Merit Scholarships.

Prerequisites: Courses, test scores, and/or grade-level classes that must be completed before taking a specific course

Prior-Prior Year (PPY): Refers to a financial aid policy that allows families to use tax information from two years ago when filing the FAFSA (Free Application for Federal Student Aid)

Private College (Independent College): A school that is not supported by state taxes

Profile: Supplementary College Board financial aid document required by some private universities

Qualified Acceptance: Occasionally, an institution postpones action on an application and will suggest that the applicant pursue a particular course in its summer session. Upon satisfactory completion of this course, the college agrees to accept the student for its regular degree programs at the beginning of the first or second semester.

Rolling Admissions: This means that a college gives an admissions decision as soon as possible after an application is completed and does not specify a notification deadline. Usually, it is wise to apply early to such colleges, since applications are usually not accepted once the admissions quota has been reached.

Reserve Officer Training Corps (ROTC): Many colleges have units of the Reserve Officer Training Corps that offer two- and four-year programs of military training culminating in an officer's commission. In some colleges, credit for the courses can be applied toward a degree. ROTC scholarships are available, which pay for full college costs.

Student Aid Index (SAI): The information you input on the Free Application for Federal Student Aid, or FAFSA, about you and your family's financial profile will determine your SAI. The index will equal the sum of your parents' available income, your income and assets. {Source: https://www.nerdwallet.com/article/loans/student-loans/what-is-the-student-aid-index)

SAT Test: A college admission exam measuring critical reading and math reasoning skills; also includes a writing section with multiple-choice questions and an essay

SAT Subject Tests (formerly called the SAT II): One-hour exams offered in 20 different subjects; required by some schools and/or some majors. Check each school's requirements carefully. Up to three SAT subject tests may be taken in one sitting.

Scholarship: A gift of money (which does not need to be repaid) given to recognize student achievement, skills, and talent; it may be based partly on financial need.

State and Regional College Tuition Discounts: The most common tuition discounts given based on residency are: Academic Common Market, Western Undergraduate Exchange, Midwest Student Exchange, Tuition Break for NE Residents.

Statement of Intent to Register (SIR): This form must be returned to the college of the student's choice by a specified date (usually the beginning of May); it confirms the student's intent to register at the college and reserves a spot.

Student Aid Report (SAR): A form distributed by the College Scholarship Service for the purpose of estimating the family contribution or SAI to a student's college costs

Test of English as a Foreign Language (TOEFL): An English language exam for foreign students used for admission purposes and for placement in college English classes

Transcript: An official copy of the high school or college grades earned by a student

Transfer Courses: College courses that may be transferred to another college

Transfer Major: Students who intend to transfer to a four-year college pursue a transfer major at a community college. This consists of the lower-division requirements for a major at a particular college.

Transfer Students: College students who transfer from one college to another, usually at the end of the sophomore year; changing colleges during the junior or senior year, when the student is completing major requirements, is not recommended.

Tuition: The fee for instruction at a college or vocational school

Unit: A fixed amount of scholastic study used as a basis for calculating academic credits; college units for a course often equal the number of hours per week the course meets. You must earn a specific number of units to receive a degree.

Undergraduate: A college student who has not yet received a bachelor's degree

Upper Division: The courses usually taken during the last two years of a four-year college program; the courses typically are advanced courses in one's major and other areas.

Waitlist: In addition to accepting and rejecting applicants, many colleges place students on a waitlist for admission. As accepted applicants decide to attend other colleges, the school will offer their places to students on the waitlist.

Weighted Courses: A policy that rewards accelerated and/or advanced work such as AP, IB, and Honors courses by awarding a "bonus" grade point for them

Work Study: A federally funded program that makes part-time jobs available to students with financial need. The earnings are taxable.

Made in the USA
Columbia, SC
05 April 2022